INTERACTIONS 5

Western Canadian Edition

JACK HOPE

MARIAN SMALL

Consultants

Valeen Chow
Ralph Connelly
Larry Elchuck
Peggy Hill
Alexander Norrie
Deborah Tempest
Sheila Tossell

ESL Consultant

Wendy McDonell

Prentice Hall Ginn Canada

INTERACTIONS 5

Canadian Cataloguing in Publication Data

Main entry under title:
Hope, Jack
   Interactions 5

Rev. ed.
Includes index.
ISBN 0-13-858499-0

1. Mathematics - Juvenile literature.   I. Small, Marian
II. Title.

QA107. H675 1997   510   C96-932601-7

ISBN 0-13-858499-0

Prentice Hall, Inc., Englewood Cliffs, New Jersey
Prentice Hall International, Inc., London
Prentice Hall of Australia, Pty., Ltd., Sydney
Prentice Hall of India Pvt., Ltd., New Delhi
Prentice Hall of Japan, Inc., Tokyo
Prentice Hall of Southeast Asia (PTE) Ltd., Singapore
Editora Prentice Hall do Brasil Ltda., Rio de Janeiro
Prentice Hall Hispanoamericana, S.A., Mexico

PUBLISHER   MaryLynne Meschino

MANAGING EDITOR   Bonnie Di Malta

EDITORS   Jacqueline Williams, Marlene Elliott, Shirley Corriveau

ART/DESIGN   Sandi Meland Cherun/Word & Image Design Studio,
ArtPlus Limited Design Consultants

Printed and bound in Canada

A   B   C   D   E   F   G – ML – 01   00   99   98   97

Contents

viii

UNIT 1

Investigating Our School

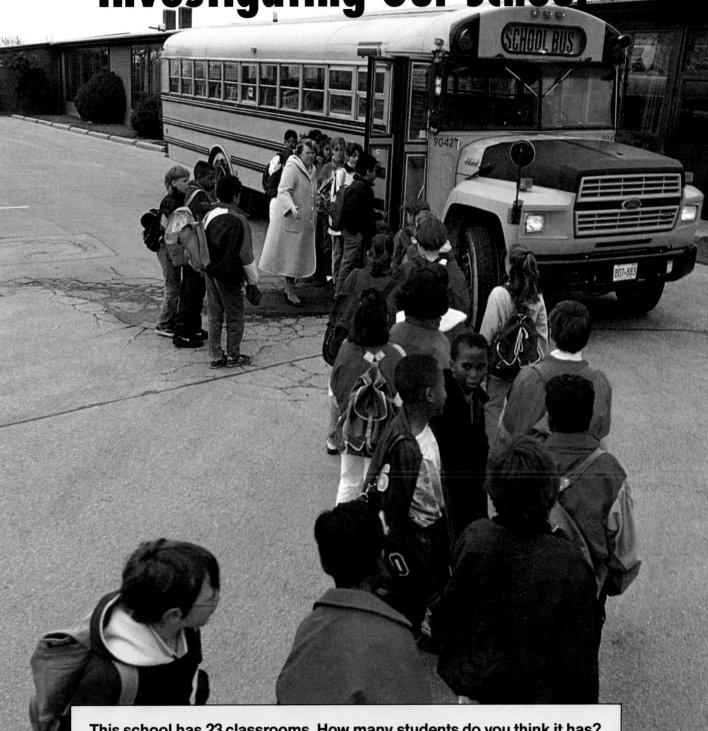

This school has 23 classrooms. How many students do you think it has?
About how many school buses would be needed for all the students in
this school to go on a field trip?
Would your school need more or fewer buses?

WHAT Do Schedules Tell Us?

Fiona studies her class schedule.

Room 15	Monday	Tuesday	Wednesday	Thursday	Friday
8:30-9:00	French	→	→	→	→
9:00-10:00	Language Arts	→	→	→	→
10:00-10:30	Phys. Ed.	Music	Phys. Ed.	Music	Language Arts
10:30-10:45	Break				
10:45-11:45	Math	→	→	→	→
11:45-12:45	Lunch				
12:45-1:00	Silent Reading	→	→	→	→
1:00-2:00	Environmental Studies	→	→	→	→
2:00-3:00	Creative Writing/ Drama	Library	Health	Art	Creative Writing/ Drama

1. How many hours is Fiona at school each day? each week?

2. How many hours of French does Fiona have each week? Estimate how many hours of French she has in the school year.

3. In one week, Fiona spends five times as many hours on math as on art. How many times as many hours does she spend on math as on French?

2

4. How much time is free time each day? About what fraction of the school day is free time?

Work in a group.

5. Use your class schedule. Compare it to Fiona's schedule. How are they the same? How are they different? How many hours do you spend at school each day? each week? each year?

6. Estimate what fraction of the school week you spend on any three subjects.

7. Draw a graph to show the number of hours spent each week on each subject in your schedule. Predict the number of hours your class would like to spend on each subject each week. How would you word the question to find out what you want to know?

8. Write questions to find out which subjects are the most and the least favorite of Grade 5 students. Predict the results.

9. For Problem 8, write out a plan for investigation which includes the following — collecting the data, recording the data, displaying the data. Then, carry out the investigation and report on the reasonableness of the results.

Did you Know...?

Schools in Moncton sometimes have to close because of winter storms.

► One school is closed for ten storm days. Is this more or less than 0.1 of the school year? How do you know?

HOW Do We Write the Date and Time?

1. Do you think the date and time on the poster are clear? Explain.

   We can use **SI notation** to write the date and time.

   March 5, 1997 at 8:15 pm would be

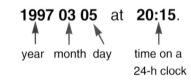

   1997 03 05 at **20:15**.

   year month day   time on a
                            24-h clock

2. SI time notation is written with 4 digits. Use SI notation to write 8:15 am.

Work with a partner.

3. Use SI notation to write the time and date if the meeting was

   May 3 at 8:15 am.   May 3 at 8:15 pm.

4. Use SI notation to write
   • today's date and the present time   • your birthdate
   • the start and end of lunch period   • start of morning recess
   • the time school ends each day   • a date that is special to you

5. Why is it important to have a standard way to write the time and date?

4

When Are We a Population and When Are We a Sample?

Timberlea School was randomly chosen to take part in a survey.

Every Timberlea student was asked what their favorite Canadian author was.

The results will be used to answer the survey question, "What is the favorite author of elementary students in the city?"

The Timberlea students are the survey's **sample**.

The city's elementary students make up the survey's **total population**.

1. Why do you think all the students in the city weren't asked?

2. Why do you think the term **sample** is a good one?

3. When is it fair to use the results from a sample to make a prediction about a population?

4. Design a survey question for which your school might be

   • a sample.   • the total population.

Work in a group.

5. Make up a survey question for which your class would be

   • a sample.   • the total population.

6. Your school needs to choose two school colors to be used on things such as uniforms and school banners.

   Design a survey question.
   Describe the total population.
   What sample might you use to answer your question?

7. When might it be possible to survey a total population rather than just a sample?

WHAT's in a Floor Plan?

Caitlin and Tai drew a floor plan of their classroom and a floor plan of the school.

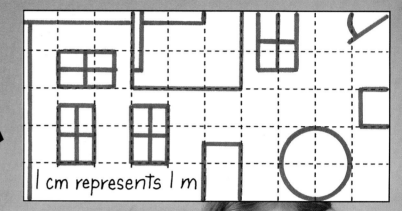

1 cm represents 1 m

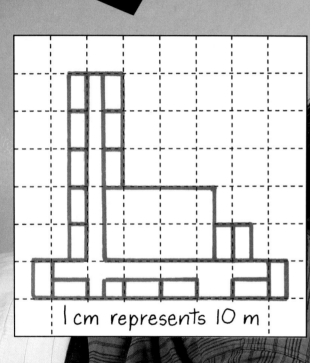

1 cm represents 10 m

1. Which floor plan is for the classroom? the school? How can you tell?

2. How are the floor plans alike? different?

3. Which floor plan has the **scale** 1 cm represents 1 m?
   What do you think this means?
   What is the scale on the other floor plan? Explain what this means.

4. About how many teacher's desks would it take to cover the floor of the classroom?

5. About what fraction of the area of the whole school is the classroom?

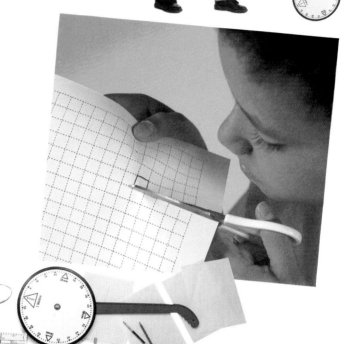

6. Discuss how to make a floor plan of your classroom. Decide
   · what measurements you need
   · what tools you need
   · what scale to use
   Draw the floor plan on grid paper.

7. Draw the desks, tables, and other furniture on grid paper. Use the same scale as the floor plan.
   Cut out the furniture pieces and place them on the floor plan of your classroom.

   Estimate what fraction of the floor area of your classroom is covered by furniture.

8. Work with another group to make a floor plan of your school.
   Describe how you made decisions about what measurements, tools, and scales to use in your group.
   Describe any problems you had in making the floor plan.

9. Using the floor plan of your school, find the shortest route from your classroom to an exit. Why is this important to know?

10. Which room in your school holds the most students?
    Will it hold all of the people in your school?

Did you know...?

A school in India once had an enrolment of 12 350 students.

▶ How many students are in your school? About how many times as many students were there in the school in India? Estimate the number of classrooms in that school.

How Do We Locate Points on a Grid?

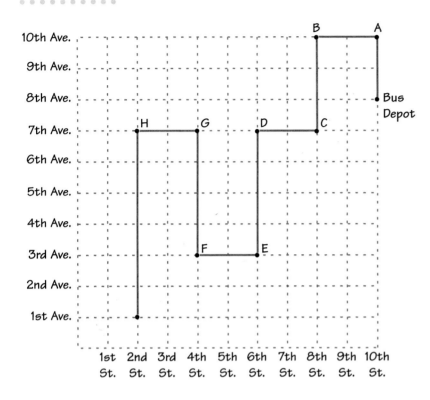

St. Ann School is located at the corner of 2nd St. and 1st Ave.

The **coordinates** (2,1) can be used to locate the school.

1. What does the first number in (2,1) represent? What about the second number?

2. What streets meet at these coordinates?
   (9,2) (2,9) (8,4) (4,8)

The route for bus #1 is shown. The letters indicate the bus stops.

3. What are the coordinates of each bus stop?

4. Nine city blocks is about 1 km. About what distance does the bus travel one way?

5. Use coordinates to describe the shortest route the bus might take to return to the bus depot.
   How much shorter is the return route compared to the bus route?

This map shows the rural school Riverbend Elementary at A (6,0), and one of its bus routes.

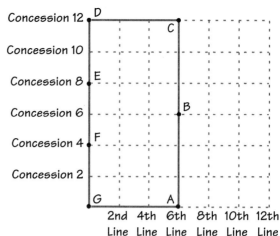

6. What roads meet at these coordinates?
   (10,2) (2,10) (8,4) (4,8)

7. What are the coordinates of each bus stop?

8. The distance between roads shown on the map is 1 km. How long is the bus route?

9. Bus stop B is to be moved to (10,6). Copy the map and draw the new route.
   What's the length of the new route?
   Is there more than one possible new route? Explain.

10. Draw straight lines to connect A,E, and C. What shape is formed?

11. Plot point H (10,8). Point H is one corner of a trapezoid. What might be the coordinates of the other corners?

12. Copy and complete this grid.

    Plot points A(60,0), B(90,40), C(50,80), and D(10,50).

    Join them with straight lines to outline a shape.
    Describe the shape.

13. Change points B and C to make a rectangle. What are the new coordinates of B and C?

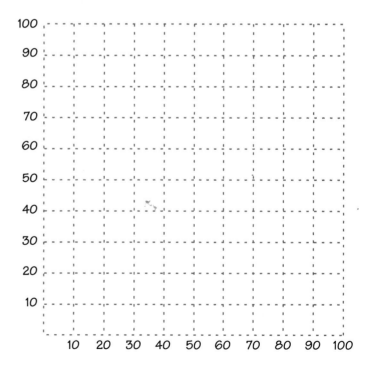

?! I Wonder...!?

Where Does Your School Rank?

Find out about the enrolment of other schools nearby. Is your school's enrolment one of the greatest, least, or in the middle?

Searching the Past

How many teachers have taught at your school since it opened? How many principals has it had? In what year did it have the most students? Write the date your school opened in SI notation.

Fundraising

How much money would each student in the school have to raise for the school to buy
- 50 library books?
- a microscope?
- a VCR?
- a computer?
- a gym set for the playground?

Who Knows?

Conduct a survey to find out if adults know how to record the date in SI notation.
- What is your question?
- What is the total population?
- What will be your sample?

How Far Away?

How many times do you have to walk around your school to go farther than 10 km? How many times do you have to walk up and down the halls to go the same distance?

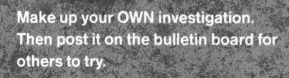

Make up your OWN investigation. Then post it on the bulletin board for others to try.

Thinking Back

One school raised enough money to cover the gym floor with coins. What information do you need to figure out how much money that would be?

It takes 800 children holding hands to go around a school.
How could you decide if the school is a large one or a small one? Explain.

Describe some situations where knowing how to read coordinates might be useful.

How would you explain to a friend how to

- change time in SI notation back to a 12-h clock.
- write a date in SI notation

Describe a survey question for which all the Grade 5 students in your community would be considered
- a sample
- the total population

INFO!

What else would you like to know about your school? Describe what you would do to find out.

▼ Show 5 different ways to arrange 48 chairs in equal rows.

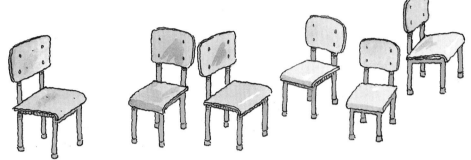

Write an addition sentence for this. ▶

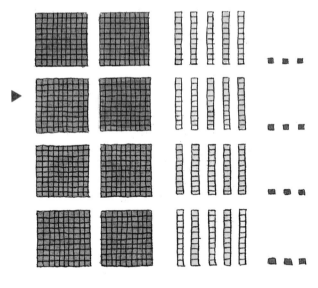

▼ How many bars of soap might be packed in this box? Explain.

Multiplication

▼ What might this table be describing?

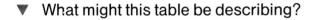

Distance Travelled

Time (hours)	1	2	3	4
Distance (kilometres)	90	180	270	360

How can you use the table to find the distance travelled in 5 hours?

◀ Think about all the times you ate yesterday. About how many plates, bowls, knives, forks, spoons, and glasses did you use?
Estimate how many of these things are washed in one month for your meals.

Draw a pentagon. Connect the vertices not already connected by sides. Do you think this action always creates a star in a pentagon? What shape is in the centre of the star?

Using Counters to Make Arrays
Recognizing multiples, factors, composites, and primes

Jeanine has made an array using 12 counters.

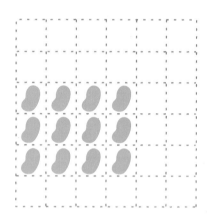

The multiplication sentence 3 x 4 = 12 describes Jeanine's array.

The numbers 3 and 4 are called **factors**.

The number 12 is the product. It is also a **multiple** of 3 and of 4.

1. Arrange 12 counters on a grid in a different array.
   Write the multiplication sentence.
   What are the factors?

2. Arrange the 12 counters in another array. What is the multiplication sentence?
   What are the factors?

   A **composite number** is a number that has more than 2 factors.

3. Is 12 a composite number? Explain.

4. Make an array to model 3 × 5 = 15.
   What are the factors? What is the multiple?

5. Make another array of 15 counters. What is the multiplication sentence?

6. Is 15 a composite number? Explain.

7. Jeanine has added 2 columns to show that 18 and 21 are also multiples of 3. List 5 other multiples of 3.

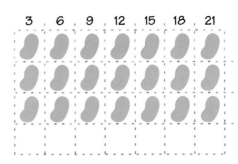

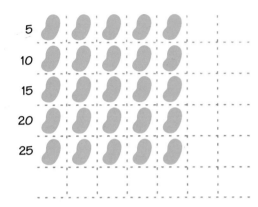

8. Jeanine has added 2 more rows to show that 20 and 25 are also multiples of 5. List 5 other multiples of 5.

9. How can you use multiplication to find 5 multiples of 4?
How can you use addition to find 5 multiples of 6?

10. Arrange 24 counters in as many arrays as you can.
Is 24 a composite number? Explain.

11. Arrange 11 counters in as many arrays as you can.
Is 11 a composite number? Explain.

A number that has exactly 2 factors is a **prime number**.
5 is a prime number because its only factors are 1 and 5.

The number 1 is neither prime nor composite.

12. Copy the following Carroll diagrams. Sort the numbers 1 to 20 according to the rules listed.

	composite	not composite
even		
odd		

	prime	not prime
factor of 12		
not a factor of 12		

13. Make up your own Carroll diagram. Challenge a classmate to use it to sort numbers.

Start with 99. Try to get to 100 by only adding 11s and subtracting 7s.

Arranging Mail Boxes

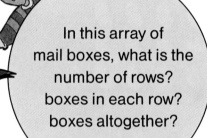

In this array of mail boxes, what is the number of rows? boxes in each row? boxes altogether?

Explain how each sentence shows the number of mail boxes.

$5 \times 8 = 40$ $8 \times 5 = 40$ $4 \times 8 + 8 = 40$

factors   product

Work with a partner.

Use connecting cubes or grid paper.

1. Show a different rectangular array of 40 boxes.
   Write two multiplication sentences for it.

2. How many boxes are in each rectangular array?
   6 rows of 5 boxes
   7 rows of 4 boxes
   8 rows of 8 boxes

3. How many rectangular arrays of 17 boxes can you make? What other numbers of boxes less than 50 form exactly this number of rectangular arrays?

4. How many boxes are in each rectangular array if one more row is added to each?

9 rows of 10 boxes
4 rows of 25 boxes
7 rows of 5 boxes

5. Tell how the first number of boxes can help you find the second number of boxes.

5 rows of 6 = 30 boxes
6 rows of 6 = [?]

4 rows of 8 = 32 boxes
4 rows of 7 = [?]

8 rows of 20 = 160 boxes
16 rows of 20 = [?]

6. Three pieces of mail like these are placed in each of these empty mail boxes. How many pieces of mail are there altogether?

7. Create and solve a problem about an equal number of pieces of mail being placed in a rectangular array of boxes.

8. 35 boxes are in a rectangular array. If there was one less row, how many boxes might there be?

9. 56 boxes are in a rectangular array. If there was one more row, how many boxes might there be?

10. Find examples of other things in rectangular arrays. Tell how to use multiplication to find the number of things in all.

The tallest man who ever lived was 272 cm tall. Estimate and then check whether he could walk upright through your classroom doorway.
How much taller than you was he?

Eating Shadows

Jule Ann found a little, dark thing in the cookie jar. The small dark thing ate Jule Ann's shadow and got a little bigger. It ate her mother's shadow and got a little bigger. It ate the toaster's shadow and got even bigger.
  "I think it's a dark," said Jule Ann.
  By this time the dark was as big as the toaster.

from *The Dark* by Robert N. Munsch

The Dark grew about 1 toaster high when it ate 3 shadows.
Suppose the Dark always grows at the same rate.
How many shadows would it have to eat to be 2 toasters high?
10 toasters high?

Work in a group.

1. Complete a table like this.

Toasters high	1	2	3	?	5	6	?	?	?	10
Shadows eaten	3	?	?	12	?	?	?	?	?	?

Explain how to find the number of shadows eaten by the Dark if you know how many toasters high it is.

2. The toaster is about 21 cm high.
  Complete a table like this.

Shadows eaten	1	2	3	?	?	?	?	?	?	10
Centimetres high	?	?	21	?	?	?	?	?	?	?

Explain how the height in centimetres of the Dark is related to the number of shadows it has eaten.

18

3. Estimate how many centimetres high the Dark will be after eating 30 shadows.

4. Estimate how many shadows the Dark must eat to be as high as a house.

5. Suppose the Dark grew at different rates. Copy and complete the table for each rate.

Toasters high	1	2	3	4	5	6	7	8	9	10
Shadows eaten	4	?	?	?	?	24	?	?	?	40

Toasters high	1	2	3	4	5	6	7	8	9	10
Shadows eaten	?	18	?	?	?	?	?	72	?	?

Toasters high	1	2	3	4	5	6	7	8	9	10
Shadows eaten	?	?	?	?	?	6	?	?	9	?

Toasters high	1	2	3	4	5	6	7	8	9	10
Shadows eaten	?	?	?	24	?	?	?	48	?	?

In each table, how are the numbers in each pair related?

6. In which table did the Dark grow the fastest? the slowest? Explain.

7. We can describe 1 toaster high for every 3 shadows eaten as a **ratio** 1 to 3 or 1 : 3. Write a ratio for each table.

8. Explain this bar graph. What would be the heights of the next three bars?

Examine the graph and your *Centimetres high* table from Problem 2. In which is the Dark growing faster? Explain.

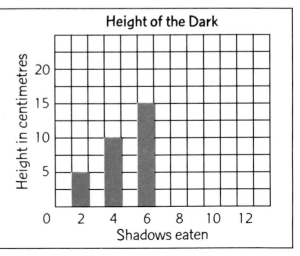

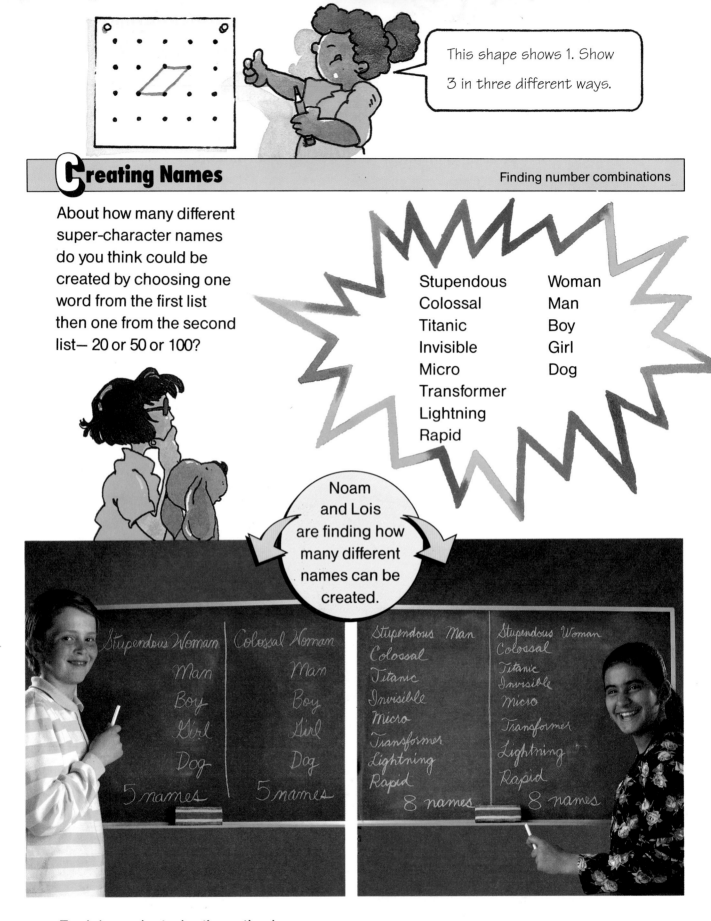

This shape shows 1. Show 3 in three different ways.

Creating Names

About how many different super-character names do you think could be created by choosing one word from the first list then one from the second list— 20 or 50 or 100?

Stupendous   Woman
Colossal   Man
Titanic   Boy
Invisible   Girl
Micro   Dog
Transformer
Lightning
Rapid

Noam and Lois are finding how many different names can be created.

Stupendous Woman | Colossal Woman
Man | Man
Boy | Boy
Girl | Girl
Dog | Dog
5 names | 5 names

Stupendous Man | Stupendous Woman
Colossal | Colossal
Titanic | Titanic
Invisible | Invisible
Micro | Micro
Transformer | Transformer
Lightning | Lightning
Rapid | Rapid
8 names | 8 names

Explain each student's method.
Finish their work. Was your estimate close?

1. Explain how multiplication could be used to find the number of names.

20

2. Add a word to the first list. How many more names can be created? Why? Write a multiplication sentence to show the total number of names that can be created.

3. Add a word to the second list. How many names can be created using this list and the first list with its extra word? Write a multiplication sentence.

4. How many words might be in each list to make each number of super-character names?

- 64
- an even number
- an odd number
- between 50 and 60
- greater than 100

5. By using the list below you can create 3-word names like Mighty Stupendous Woman. How many 3-word names can be created using this list and the two original lists? Write a multiplication sentence.

Mighty
Thundering
Dynamic
Invincible

6. Add two words to the new list in Problem 5. Write a multiplication sentence to show the number of 3-word names that can be made using this list and the two original lists.

7. How many different names can be made using the first and last names in your group? your class?

Take Your Pick

ODD SUMS

What do you notice about the sums in this pattern?

1 + 3
1 + 3 + 5
1 + 3 + 5 + 7
1 + 3 + 5 + 7 + 9

Write the addition that shows the product of 12 and 12.

FAVORITE MEAL

Yum·Yum·Yum

List a few of your favorite main courses, desserts, and drinks. How many different meals (main course, dessert, and drink) can you form using the favorites you listed?

100 BEAN SALAD

A 100 bean salad is made with kidney beans and string bean pieces. It has 3 times as many string bean pieces as kidney beans. How many of each type of bean are used?

PLOTTING FACTORS

The numbers in the ordered pair (4, 6) multiply to give a product of 24.

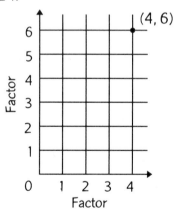

Plot all the ordered pairs that have 24 as the product of the numbers. Describe the shape made by the dots. Plot the factors of 36 and then of 48. What do you notice about each shape?

TRAVELLING ANTS

Three ants leave the corner of a centimetre grid and walk continuously in different routes. One always walks 1 cm right and 2 cm up. Another always walks 2 cm right and 4 cm up. The third always walks 2 cm right and 1 cm up. Do their paths ever cross? Explain.

Make up other problems. Post them on the bulletin board for your classmates to solve.

22

Find two ways to continue this pattern.
5, 25, . . .

Rearranging Marching Bands

By marching in place, 6 rows of 15 band players become 3 groups of 30.

Factors of 90	
1 × ☐ = 90	5 × ☐ = 90
2 × ☐ = 90	6 × 15 = 90
3 × 30 = 90	9 × ☐ = 90

What other equal groups are possible for 90 band players? Complete the chart.

Work in a group.

Draw diagrams. Use grid paper if you wish.

1. Show each band. Rearrange each into equal groups in different ways. Write a multiplication sentence for each way.

   4 × 25   6 × 20   6 × 30

2. Find 2 different ways to rearrange 4 rows of 60 players into equal groups.

3. Find different ways to rearrange these players into equal groups.

   4 rows of 80   8 rows of 50   6 rows of 70

4. The largest marching band has 4524 members. Find two different ways to rearrange this band into equal groups.

What two consecutive page numbers in this book have a sum of 357? a product of 342?

Going to the Bank

Joel is depositing seven $20 bills and four $50 bills. He counts. Then he checks by multiplying.

Complete Joel's work for four $50 bills.

20, 40, 60, 80, 100, 120, 140

Work in a group.

Use play money.

1. Find the amount of each deposit.

   • 8 × $10   • 9 × $20   • 7 × $50   • 9 × $100

$20	2 tens
× 7	× 7
	14 tens
	or 140

2. Complete each pattern. Make up a similar multiplication pattern.

   | 6 × $10 |
   | 6 × $100 |
   | 6 × $1000 |

   | 7 × $4 |
   | 7 × $40 |
   | 7 × $400 |

   | 9 × $2 |
   | 9 × $20 |
   | 9 × $200 |

3. Show how the first deposit helps you find the others.

   | 7 × $10 = $70 |
   | 7 × $20 |
   | 7 × $50 |

   | 5 × $10 = $50 |
   | 5 × $20 |
   | 5 × $200 |

4. Roll a die to find the number of each bill to deposit. Then find the total of the deposit.

   ? × $5
   ? × $10
   ? × $20
   ? × $50
   ? × $100

5. Which bills when counted or multiplied always have totals that end in zero?

6. Joel deposited $240 of the same type of bills. How many bills might he have deposited?

How old are people three times as old as you? How old will they be when you are as old as they are now?

Doing Estimation Experiments

About how many breaths do you take in a day? To find out, Ralph and Laurie did an experiment.

1 minute is up.

16 times in 1 minute
60 minutes in 1 hour
24 hours in 1 day

Ralph estimates 16 × 60 × 24. 16 × 60 is about 20 × 50 = 1000	Laurie estimates 16 × 60 × 24. 16 × 24 is about 16 × 25 = 4 × 100 = 400

Finish their estimates.
Why does Laurie multiply 16 and 24 before multiplying by 60?
Find another way to estimate 16 × 60 × 24.

Work with a partner.

Estimate and explain what you do.

1. Suppose you could snap your fingers as fast as possible from the time you arrive at school until it is time to go home. About how many times would you snap your fingers?

2. About how long would it take to print by hand one of your favorite books?

3. About how far would you walk in a month if you walked quickly for 15 minutes at lunch each school day?

If you couldn't find a calendar, how could you find the day of the week that today's date will be next year?

Counting Windows

The front wall of an 8-floor building has 19 windows on each floor.
How many windows are in the wall?

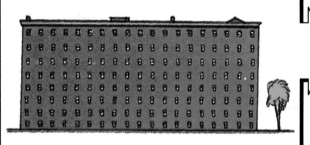

Kim uses grid paper.
She shows 8 × 20 and then removes the 20th column.

$$\begin{array}{r} 19 \\ \times\ 8 \\ \hline \cancel{160} \end{array}$$

Finish Kim's calculation.
Show another way to find the number of windows.

Work in a group.

Use grid paper or base ten blocks.

1. How does the multiplication sentence help you find each number of windows?

   8 × 50 = 400
   8 floors of 51 windows
   8 floors of 48 windows

2. Find each number of windows.

   7 floors of 29
   6 floors of 18
   5 floors of 39

3. A building has 4 floors of 19 windows on each of 4 walls. If you owned a window washing company, what would you charge to wash one window? all the windows in the building?

4. Complete each set.
   What patterns do you notice?

2 × 99
3 × 99
4 × 99
5 × 99

2 × 999
3 × 999
4 × 999
5 × 999

5. Show how to use multiplication to find the total number of windows in a large building you know.

Take Your Pick

BROKEN KEY

How could you find each product on a calculator with a broken $\boxed{9}$ key?

7×99

12×998

9×555

MAKE A THOUSAND

Find pairs of numbers that have a product of 1000. Can you find any without zeros in them?

COUNTING "THE"

About how many times is the word *the* used in one of your favorite books? Tell what you did to estimate.

COIN BALANCING

The tallest single column of coins ever stacked on the edge of another coin was 205 Canadian quarters on the edge of a Canadian Olympic coin.

Estimate the height of the column. Tell what you did.

MAGIC NUMBERS

- Use any number.

  $\boxed{?} \times 8 \times 125$

Try some other numbers. How are the products alike? Explain why.

Make up other problems. Post them on the bulletin board for your classmates to solve.

Use a calculator to find each product.

11 × 11   11 × 12   11 × 13   11 × 14

Describe a pattern that can help you multiply by 11.

$\mathcal{S}$elling Newspaper Ads

Comparing algorithms

Katja, Simone, and some friends publish a neighborhood newspaper. They sell advertising space in it.

> FOR SALE boy's bike, used 6 mos; girl's figure skates, size 4; bunk beds; men's cross-country skis; many more sports items; phone 555-0583 after 6.

Each symbol and space in an ad is considered a character. The cost of an ad depends upon the number of characters. Advertisers print their ads on grid forms.

Katja uses the grid to find the cost of this 147-character ad at 6¢ per character.

Please print clearly one character per space.

F	O	R		S	A	L	E		b	o	y	'	s		b	i	k	e	,20
	u	s	e	d		b		m	o	s	;		g	i	r	l	'	s	40
f	i	g	u	r	e		s	k	a	t	e	s	,		s	i	z	e	60
4	;		b	u	n	k		b	e	d	s	;		m	e	n	'	s	80
c	r	o	s	s	-	c	o	u	n	t	r	y		s	k	i	s	;	100
m	a	n	y		m	o	r	e		s	p	o	r	t	s		i	t	e 120
m	s	;		p	h	o	n	e		5	5	5	-	0	5	8	3		a 140
f	t	e	r		6	.													160

} 100 × 6¢ = 600¢

} 40 × 6¢ = 240¢

} 7 × 6¢ = 42¢

Finish Katja's work.

```
  H T O
      4
  1 4 7        6 × 7 pennies = 42 pennies
×     6        42 pennies = [4] dimes, [2] pennies
  ─────
     [2]

  H T O
 [2] 4
  1 4 7        6 × 4 dimes + 4 dimes = 28 dimes
×     6        28 dimes = [2] dollars, [8] dimes
  ─────
 [8] 2
```

Simone uses a place value chart to find the cost of the ad.

Finish Simone's work.

Is this another way to help find the cost? Explain.

```
 2 4
147
× 6
───
 82
```

Work in a group.

Model your solutions.

1. Find the cost of each of these ads at 7¢ per character.

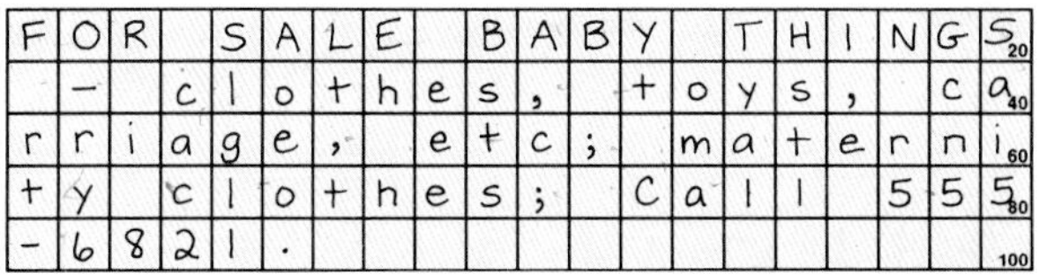
FOR SALE BABY THINGS
— clothes, toys, ca
rriage, etc; materni
ty clothes; Call 555
-6821.

MOVING SALE beds, dr
essers, fridge, free
zer, washer, dryer,
desk, TV, etc. Great
Prices! 12 Maple Av
e. Sat. 9:30-2.

2. Find the cost of each of these ads.
   - 135 characters at 6¢ per character
   - 216 characters at 4¢ per character
   - 555 characters at 5¢ per character

3. The cost of this ad at 8¢ per character is being found. Explain and finish this method.

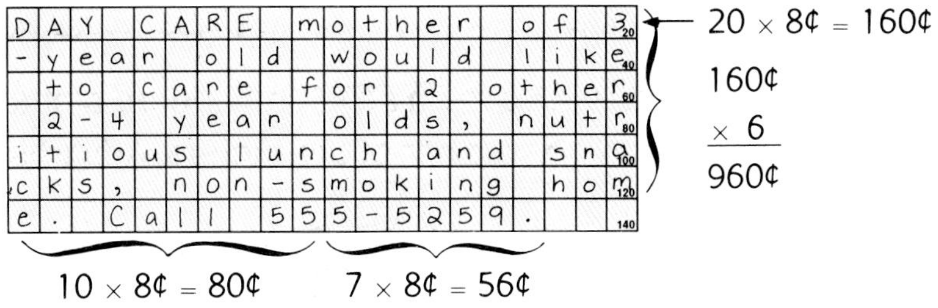
DAY CARE mother of 3
-year old would like
to care for 2 other
2-4 year olds, nutr
itious lunch and sna
cks, non-smoking hom
e. Call 555-5259.
20 × 8¢ = 160¢
160¢
× 6
960¢
10 × 8¢ = 80¢
7 × 8¢ = 56¢

4. The cost of an ad is found.

$$\begin{array}{r} {\scriptstyle 2\,2} \\ 145 \\ \times\ 5¢ \\ \hline 725¢ \end{array}$$

Then the advertiser adds 10 characters. How can you find the cost without starting over?

5. Which of these ads cost less than $10? Explain what you did.
   - 245 characters at 5¢ per character
   - 129 characters at 6¢ per character
   - 345 characters at 3¢ per character

6. Find the cost of a 157-character ad at this price.
   - 5¢ per character for the first 100 characters
   - 3¢ per character after the first 100 characters

7. An ad had 264 characters. What price per character was charged for the cost to be about $13?

FOR SALE

8. Make up an ad with more than 100 characters. Ask another group to set the price per character and find the cost.

9. Investigate the cost of advertising in a local paper. Find an ad and estimate its cost.

What do you need to add to 427 so that when you subtract 8216 from the sum, you get 100?

Examining Crossword Puzzles

Sergio and Lynne are finding the number of squares in this crossword puzzle by multiplying.

Sergio uses the puzzle.

Finish his work.

Make a frame.

Fill it in.

Remove the frame and find the result.

Lynne uses base ten blocks. Explain how Lynne's model shows 23 × 12. Finish her work.

$$
\begin{array}{r}
23 \\
\times 12 \\
\hline
200 \\
30 \\
40 \\
6 \\
\hline
\end{array}
$$

30

1. Make a frame with base ten blocks for each crossword puzzle.

   22 rows of 36 squares
   14 rows of 51 squares
   34 × 25

Work in a group.

Use base ten blocks or grid paper.

2. Find the number of squares in each puzzle. → 7 rows of 12 squares | 12 rows of 15 squares | 18 × 24

3. Show how finding the number of squares in the first puzzle helps you find the number of squares in the others.

   15 × 15 = 225   15 × 16   14 × 15   30 × 15

```
   2 4
  ×2 4
 ─────
   9 6
   4 8
 ─────
  ☐☐☐
```

4. Which puzzle has the greatest number of squares?

   24 × 24   23 × 25   22 × 26

5. Find the number of rows in a square crossword puzzle with 256 squares.

6. How many rows are in a puzzle with 12 squares in a row and 156 squares in all?

7. Find a crossword puzzle in a book or newspaper. Show how to find the number of squares by multiplying.

1, 2, and 3 form a row on a calculator.
Subtract 123 from 321.
What do you get?
What happens if you use the keys in a different row? in a column?

Calculating Costs

Peter's class is planning a field trip. The costs of several possible trips are shown. The costs include bussing and admission.

Cost to each student	
Museum	$4.75
Zoo	$5.25
Science Centre	$6.25
Provincial Park	$4.50
Art Galley	$3.50

Peter multiplies to find out the total student cost for a trip to the science centre.

$6.25 = 625¢ so for 23 students, it will cost 23 × 625¢.

You can find the product in parts.

A. Rename the factors in hundreds + tens + ones.

23 = 20 + 3   625 = 600 + 20 + 5

B. Multiply using a table.

×	600 +	20 +	5
20 +	12 000	400	100
3	1800	60	15

C. Rename each part.
12 000 + 400 + 100 = 12 500
1800 + 60 + 15 = 1875

D. Add.
```
  12 500
+  1 875
  14 375
```

E. Estimate to check.
23 × 625 is about 20 × 700
= 20 × 7 hundreds
= 140 hundreds
= 14 000

F. Change the cents to dollars and cents.   14 375¢ = $143.75

1. Use Peter's method to find the cost for a trip to the zoo for 25 students. Estimate to check.

Janet has 30 students in her class.
She multiplied a different way.

$$
\begin{array}{r}
625 \\
\times 30
\end{array}
\quad\longrightarrow\quad
\begin{array}{r}
\overset{1}{6}25 \\
\times 3 \text{ tens} \\
\hline
1875 \text{ tens}
\end{array}
\begin{array}{l}
= 18750¢ \\
= \$187.50
\end{array}
$$

2. Use Janet's method to find the cost for 20 students to go to the museum.

Kelly's class of 20 students wants to go to the park.
She found the total cost mentally.

$$
\begin{aligned}
20 \times 450 = 10 \times 900 \quad &= 10 \times 9 \text{ hundreds} \\
&= 90 \text{ hundreds} \\
&= 9000 \\
&= \$90.00
\end{aligned}
$$

3. Use Kelly's method to find the cost for a trip to the art gallery for 20 students.

Find the total cost for each trip in Problems 4 to 7. Use any method of multiplying. Estimate to check.

4. A class of 27 students wants to go to the museum.

5. A class of 30 has decided to go to the science centre.

6. Two classes, a total of 50 students, want to go to the art gallery.

7. There are 24 students planning a trip to the zoo.

8. Create and solve multiplication problems for which you would use each of the three multiplying methods in this lesson.

Each letter represents a different digit.
Find a solution.

FOUR
+ ONE

FIVE

OVERDUES

What do I do?
What do I do?
This library book is 42
Years overdue.
I admit that it's mine
But I can't pay the fine —
Should I turn it in
Or hide it again?
What do I do?
What do I do?

from *A Light in the Attic*
by Shel Silverstein

If the fine for an overdue book
is 10¢ a day, what would
the fine be for the book?

Julian and Estelle use calculators to find the fine.

c	365	×	42	×	10

=	153300

Julian multiplies 365 and 42 to
find the number of days in
42 years. Then he multiplies
by 10.

Why does he multiply by 10?
How many dollars is 153 300¢?

34

Estelle multiplies 365 and 10 to find the fine for 1 year. Then she multiplies by 42.

Why does she multiply by 42? Why did Estelle and Julian get the same answer?

Would you pay the fine or pay for the book?

Work with a partner.

Use a calculator.

1. Show how the fine just calculated can be used to find these fines.

   - 5¢ a day for 42 years
   - 15¢ a day for 42 years
   - 25¢ a day for 42 years
   - 30¢ a day for 84 years

2. A book costs $54.95. It is overdue 1 year and 1 day at 15¢ a day. How does the fine compare to the cost of the book?

3. At 25¢ a day, the fine for a book is $55.00. Is the book overdue more or less than 6 months?

4. Estelle thought she had multiplied 15 × 365 × 42.

   The display showed $\boxed{21900}$.

   What mistake might she have made?

5. The fine at one library doubles each day a book is overdue.

Days overdue	1	2	3	4
Fine	1¢	2¢	4¢	8¢

   What is the fine for a book overdue 20 days?

6. The record for an overdue book was set when a book borrowed in 1688 was returned in 1976.
   Find out the overdue fine at your library. Estimate the fine for that book.

  **M**ultiplying

There are lots of ways to calculate 5 × 198.
Here are some. Can you think of any more?

---

1. You can multiply too much and then subtract. Model using base ten blocks.

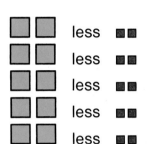

less ■■

less ■■

less ■■

less ■■

less ■■

> What do these colored squares represent?

5 × 200 = 1000 less 10 → 990

5 × 198 = 990

---

2. You might double 5 and halve 198.

double ⟨ 5 × 198 ⟩ half

10 × 99

10 × 99 = 990

5 × 198 = 990

---

3. You could multiply from the right and regroup.

```
  44
 198      5 × 8 ones → 40 → 4 tens 0 ones
 × 5      5 × 9 tens + 4 tens → 49 tens → 4 hundreds 9 tens
 ───
 990      5 × 1 hundred + 4 hundreds → 9 hundreds
```

5 × 198 = 990

---

4. You could multiply in parts and add.

```
 198
 × 5
 ───
 500      5 × 1 hundred
 450      5 × 9 tens
  40      5 × 8 ones
 ───
 990            5 × 198 = 990
```

Work in a group.

Show two different ways to do each multiplication.

1. 9 × 55   **2.** 5 × 298

3. 249   **4.** 129   **5.** 397
   × 6   × 4   × 3

36

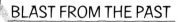

BLAST FROM THE PAST

Try this old math problem.

25 sheep are worth 5 oxen.
5 oxen are worth 2 horses.
2 horses can be bought for $100.
What is the cost of each animal?

MAKING WISHES

On Sunday Travis was granted 3 wishes.
On Monday he used each wish to wish for 3 more wishes.
On Tuesday he used each wish to wish for 3 more wishes.
How many wishes will he have by Saturday?

CALCULATOR PATTERNS

Complete each set of 3 products.

10 × 10	20 × 20	30 × 30
9 × 11	19 × 21	29 × 31
8 × 12	18 × 22	28 × 32

What patterns do you notice?

Show how you can use a pattern to find these products without a calculator.

38 × 42   51 × 49   61 × 59   72 × 68

ANOTHER WAY

Greta multiplied 45 and 23 like this.

```
     45
   × 23
  -----
     15
    120
    100
    800
  -----
   1035
```

Explain her work. Check it using base 10 blocks or a grid.
Try her method for multiplying 92 and 39.

MAGIC TRICK

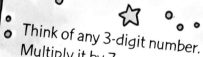

Think of any 3-digit number.
Multiply it by 7.
Then multiply the product by 11.
Finally, multiply that product by 13.
Try other 3-digit numbers.
What happens each time? Explain.

Make up other problems. Post them on the bulletin board for your classmates to solve.

Solving a Problem by Making an Organized List

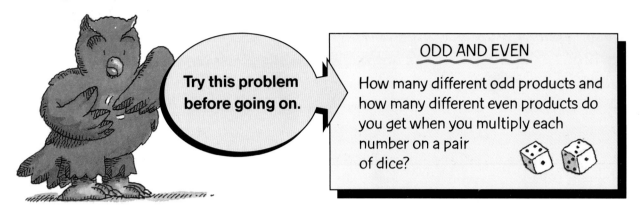

Try this problem before going on.

ODD AND EVEN

How many different odd products and how many different even products do you get when you multiply each number on a pair of dice?

Anya's group solved this problem by making an organized list.

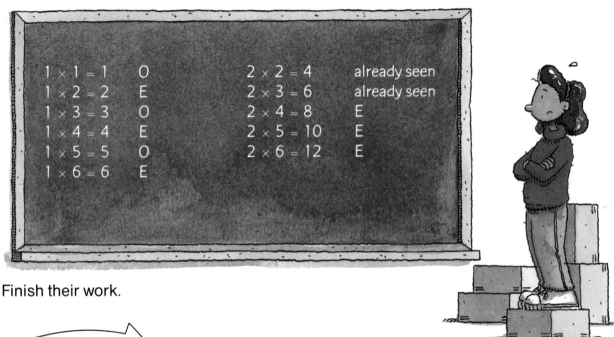

$1 \times 1 = 1$	O	$2 \times 2 = 4$	already seen
$1 \times 2 = 2$	E	$2 \times 3 = 6$	already seen
$1 \times 3 = 3$	O	$2 \times 4 = 8$	E
$1 \times 4 = 4$	E	$2 \times 5 = 10$	E
$1 \times 5 = 5$	O	$2 \times 6 = 12$	E
$1 \times 6 = 6$	E		

Finish their work.

Work in a group.

Solve these problems using an organized list.

SISTERS

The sum of the ages of two sisters is greater than the product of their ages. What could their ages be?

MATH PAGES

Which page numbers in this book can be divided evenly by both 2 and 3?

MAKING CHANGE

How many ways can you make change for a dollar using dimes and nickels?

Practising What You've Learned

Write a problem for each of these. Then solve.

1. 8 × 12   **2.** 2 × 365   **3.** 5 × 1000

4.   485
      × 7

5.   200
      × 6

6.   178
       × 8

7.   101
       × 22

8.   292
       × 13

9.   165
       × 35

10.   109
        × 19

Solve. Identify those that use multiplication.

11. In a year, about 12 million passengers pass through Toronto's airport while 4 million pass through Calgary's. How many more passengers pass through Toronto's airport than Calgary's?

12. An Olympic runner ran a 25 km race in less than 1 hour 14 minutes. How many metres did he run?

13. How many months will it take to brush your hair 1000 times if you brush it 3 times a day?

14. What is the date 100 days from today?

15. What would you expect to pay for the larger drink?

16. An amateur detective kit has 5 beards, 3 wigs, and 4 noses. How many different disguises can be made using one of each?

49¢

250 mL   750 mL

17. A car travels 80 km in 1 hour. About how many hours will it take to travel over 1000 km?

18. A bag of popcorn costs $1.65. About how much money is needed to buy 1 bag for every 2 students in your class?

19. Make up a multiplication sentence which has a composite product, one factor which is neither prime nor composite, and another odd factor.

Playing Games for Practice

Play each game in a group of 2, 3, or 4.

Three in a Row

- Multiply two numbers, one from each factor list.
- If the product is on the gameboard, place a counter on that square.
- Take turns. Each player uses a different color of counters.
- The winner is the first player with 3 counters side-by-side in a row, column, or diagonal (↗ or ↘).

Factor Lists

3	4
10	5
25	6
40	20
50	80
100	200
500	1000

Example
50 × 20 = 1000
Place a counter on 1000.

250	40	50	200	100
500	320	160	400	2000
1000	3000	6000	300	240
1200	600	320	125	200
8000	10 000	800	5000	150

Greatest Product

- Spin the spinner.
- Write the digit in any square in your 3-digit by 1-digit multiplication.
- Take turns until each player has a digit in each square.
- The winner is the player with the greatest product.

Example

 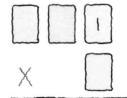

Variations: • The winner is the player with the least product.
          • Use a 2-digit by 2-digit or 2-digit by 3-digit multiplication.

40

RACING SNAIL

A garden snail named Verne completed a 31 cm course in a record time of 2 minutes 13 seconds.
Estimate how long it would take Verne to travel the length of your classroom. About how many times as fast as Verne's time is your walking time?

GREATER THAN 16

How many different products greater than 16 are possible when you multiply each number on a pair of dice?

CONSECUTIVE NUMBERS PRODUCT

List any 4 consecutive numbers. Multiply the first and last numbers together. Then multiply the second and third numbers together. Compare the products.
Try this with other sets of 4 consecutive numbers. What do you notice?

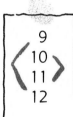

9
10
11
12

COUNTING SWALLOWS

How many times do you normally swallow when drinking a glass of water, milk, juice, or soft drink? About how many times do you swallow when drinking in a week? in a month?

CALCULATOR PATTERN

What do you notice?

$1 \times 90 + 21$
$12 \times 90 + 31$
$123 \times 90 + 41$

Make up other problems. Post them on the bulletin board for your classmates to solve.

1. How would you multiply these numbers in your head?

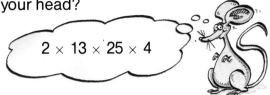

   $2 \times 13 \times 25 \times 4$

2. Estimate 410×18. Will your estimate be less than or greater than the exact answer? Tell why. Multiply to check.

3. How does knowing $11 \times 13 = 143$ help you find 22×13?

4. Tell how you know that 8×258 is greater than 2000 without finding the product.

5. A lunch special for $6.50 consists of
   - either soup of the day or a chef's salad
   - one of 4 sandwiches
   - one of 3 desserts
   - one of 4 drinks

   How many different $6.50 lunch specials are possible?

6. The world's fastest talker can speak about 450 words in a minute. About how long will it take him to speak over 5000 words?

7. Which digits can be used in the hundredths place to give a product with 3 zeros?

   $5 \times \boxed{?}00$

8. Which are worth more— 87 six-cent stamps or 105 five-cent stamps? How much more?

9. Could there be an error? How do you know?

   $\times 20 = 450$

Multiplying 300 and 40 is as easy as multiplying 3 and 4.

What does Marian mean?

Write about how multiplication and addition are alike.
Then write about how they are different.

It's always quicker to multiply large numbers on a calculator.

Not always!

List some examples to explain what Michelle means.

Karen thinks all even numbers are composite and all odd numbers are prime. List examples to explain why she's wrong.

$$\begin{array}{r} 299 \\ \times\ 4 \\ \hline 866 \end{array}$$

Write a note to Luke to tell him why his answer is not reasonable.

What questions do you still have about multiplication?

3 Examining Fractions

◄

What fraction of the letters are used in the word RUGBY?   FOOTBALL?

What fraction of all the letters are vowels?

What decimal describes the portion of all the letters that are circled?

What other fractions or decimals does this Word Search puzzle suggest?

▼ When we compare the number of green cubes in the first and second trains, we see that $\frac{3}{10} > \frac{2}{10}$.

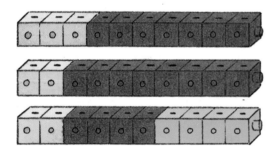

What other comparisons do the first and second trains show? Use fractions. What are you comparing?

What comparisons do the first and third trains show? Use decimals. What are you comparing?

▼ What fraction of each team are these athletes?

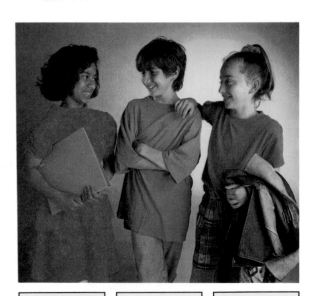

basketball	baseball	hockey
5 players	9 players	6 players

and Decimals

▼ About what fraction of all the students does each colored section represent?

What Is Your
Favorite Fast Food?

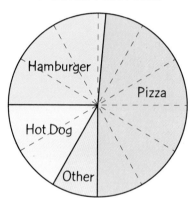

▲ This shape is $\frac{1}{2}$ of another shape.

What might the other shape be?
What if this shape was $\frac{1}{3}$ of another?
$\frac{1}{5}$ of another?

Would you use a fraction or a decimal to describe each situation? Explain.
- a length of ribbon between 16 cm and 17 cm
- the portion of a family of 10 that are adults
- the portion of your class that are girls

Write a fraction or decimal sentence to describe something about yourself.

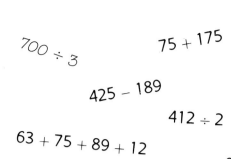

$700 \div 3$

$75 + 175$

$425 - 189$

$412 \div 2$

$63 + 75 + 89 + 12$

22×9

Without doing the calculations, decide which two answers will be closest to 200. Explain your thinking.

Using Fractions in Quilts

Mara is making a square patch that is $\frac{1}{4}$ blue, $\frac{1}{4}$ green, and $\frac{2}{4}$ yellow.

What is meant by $\frac{1}{4}$ blue?

Patchwork Designs

The shape used most often in patchwork is the square. A square patch is divided into smaller squares or triangles. The colors of the smaller shapes make a design. Sometimes the designs are given names.

Checkerboard

Windmill

Patience

Friendship Star

Tam's Patch

Mixed Squares

Simple Star

1. Design a different square patch with the same fractions of the three colors as Mara's.

2. Which of the designs show fourths?

3. Which of the designs show eighths?

4. Which design shows ninths? What other fraction does it show?

Color and cut out square patches.

5. Make part of a quilt using 3 Patience patches in blue and yellow like this.
   What fraction of one patch is one square?
   What fraction of the squares are blue in one patch?
   How many blue squares are there in total?
   How many complete patches could you make using only the blue squares?
   Cut out and rearrange the squares to show that 2 patches are blue.
   Describe the yellow squares in each patch as a fraction.

6. Make a Windmill patch in blue and green.
   How many eighths are blue?
   How many eighths are green?

7. Show what one patch of each quilt might look like.
   • 4 eighths white
   • 1 eighth blue
   • 3 eighths green
   • 3 ninths blue
   • 7 ninths red
   • 2 fourths yellow
   • 3 eighths purple
   • 3 eighths pink
   • 6 ninths yellow
   • 4 sixteenths green

8. What is unusual about this patch?
   How would you draw it?

I have 1 square patch made with 3 colors. Two parts are purple, 2 parts are yellow, and 3 parts are green.

9. Design a quilt and describe the colors using fractions.

Divide this square into 4 sets of 4 numbers.
The sum of numbers in each set must be 50.

10	9	22	7
25	16	9	16
8	16	6	21
1	11	12	11

easuring Unusual Objects

In $\frac{3}{10}$, what does the 3 mean?
the 10?

How do you read 0.3 m?

1. What fraction and decimal would
   describe the paper clip if it was
   longer by 1 dm?   20 cm?   5 cm?

2. Use a fraction and a decimal to describe the length of each giant eraser
   as a part of a metre.

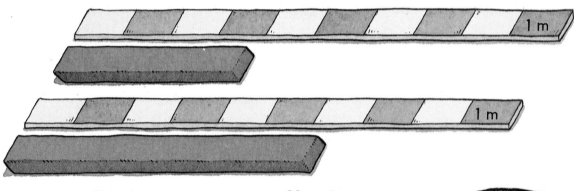

1 m

1 m

• an eraser 5 dm long   • one 82 cm long

3. Which decimal describes this running shoe —
   0.5 m or 0.05 m?
   Tell why.

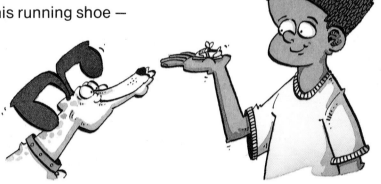

48

4. This giant soccer ball is 2.36 m across. How many centimetres across is it?

Which way do you read 2.36 m?
- 2 and 3 tenths, 6 hundredths of a metre
- 2 and 36 hundredths of a metre

5. A yo-yo is 1.82 m across. How would you read this decimal? Is this yo-yo unusually large or unusually small?

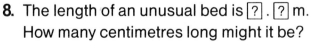

Work with a partner.

6. Make a model of each object. Describe each length in centimetres and decimetres. Is each of these objects unusually large or unusually small?
- a pencil 0.45 m long
- a pancake 0.01 m across
- a pizza 0.78 m across
- a carrot 0.83 m long

7. Cut string to each length.

4.23 m   1.2 m   0.32 m   0.04 m

For each length, describe an object that is usually that length, and an object that isn't usually that length.

8. The length of an unusual bed is ☐ . ☐ m. How many centimetres long might it be?

9. A giant basket is 1 m + 7 cm + 5 dm tall. How tall is it in metres? decimetres? centimetres?

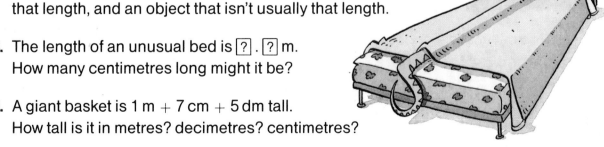

10. Find an unusual object at home. Measure it in metres. Bring in the object or a drawing with its measurements.

Draw a shape like this. Draw another line across the square in a different place. What shapes can you make?

Buying Dozens

$\frac{1}{2}$ of the doughnuts are chocolate.

$\frac{6}{12}$ of the doughnuts are chocolate.

$\frac{1}{2}$ and $\frac{6}{12}$ are **equivalent** fractions.

Why do you think they are called equivalent?

1. Write a fraction to describe each type of dessert in the whole package.

blueberry muffins   bran muffins   vanilla cookies   chocolate cookies

2. How many muffins will there be altogether in 2 packages? 3 packages?

4. How many cookies will there be altogether in 2 packages? 3 packages?

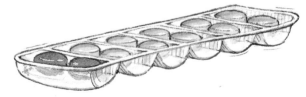

3. Write 2 equivalent fractions for each type of muffin in each number of packages.

5. Write 2 equivalent fractions for each type of cookie in each number of packages.

6. Write 2 equivalent fractions for the number of lemon tarts and the number of cherry tarts.

7. Write 2 equivalent fractions for the number of brown eggs and the number of white eggs.

Use egg cartons, dividing strips, and counters.

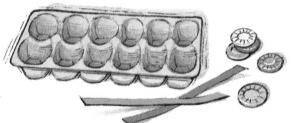

8. Show each fraction of a dozen. Then name a fraction equivalent to it.

$\frac{3}{4}$ $\frac{5}{6}$ $\frac{3}{3}$ $\frac{4}{6}$

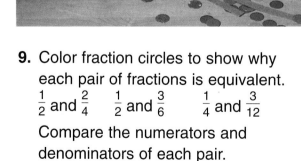

9. Color fraction circles to show why each pair of fractions is equivalent.

$\frac{1}{2}$ and $\frac{2}{4}$ $\frac{1}{2}$ and $\frac{3}{6}$ $\frac{1}{4}$ and $\frac{3}{12}$

Compare the numerators and denominators of each pair. What do you notice?

10. Make up and check a rule about the numerators and the denominators of equivalent fractions.

Does the rule work for $\frac{3}{4}$ and $\frac{9}{12}$? $\frac{2}{4}$ and $\frac{3}{6}$?

11. Find three more pairs of equivalent fractions for $\frac{1}{2}$ dozen.

12. Why might it be easier to find equivalent fractions for $\frac{1}{4}$ than for $\frac{3}{4}$?

The outline of a shape goes through 6 squares on a 10 by 10 grid. What might the shape be?

Recycling and Returning Pop Containers

Relating fractions and decimals

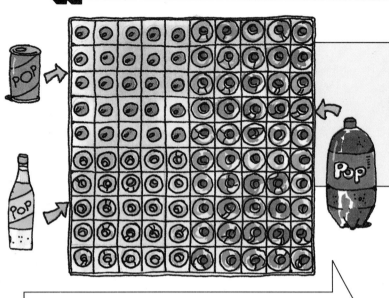

$\frac{25}{100}$, $\frac{1}{4}$, and 0.25 all describe the glass bottle portion of the box. Tell why. What decimal and fractions describe the portion that is pop cans? plastic bottles? all bottles?

1. What fractions and decimal describe the portion that is pop cans? plastic bottles? recyclable? returnable?

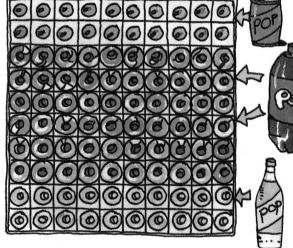

Work in a group.

Use counters and a hundredths grid as a pop container box.

2. Show each fraction of a full box. Write an equivalent fraction and decimal.

$$\frac{2}{4} \qquad \frac{3}{4} \qquad \frac{3}{5} \qquad \frac{1}{20} \qquad \frac{2}{20} \qquad \frac{1}{25}$$

3. Model the decimal that is closest to $\frac{1}{3}$ of a full box.

4. Show $\frac{1}{10}$ of a full box.

   Which of these describe how full the boxes are? Explain.

   $$\frac{10}{100} \qquad 0.1 \qquad 0.01$$

   What fractions and decimals describe the portion that is empty?

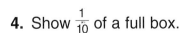

52

Take Your Pick

SPLIT UP

What fraction of the whole rectangle is each part?

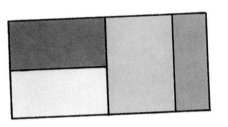

RIGHT OR WRONG?

André said that $\frac{1}{4}$ = 0.4. Is he right or wrong? Show why.

FRACTION PATTERNS

What are the next two fractions?
Create a similar pattern of your own.
What type of fractions are these fractions?

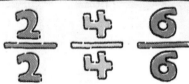

MEASURING HAIR

A human hair is about 0.07 mm wide. About how many hairs placed side-by-side would measure 1 mm? 1 cm? 1 dm? 1 m?

DECIMAL PATTERNS

Continue the pattern for 4 more fractions.

$\frac{1}{20}$ = 0.005 $\frac{2}{20}$ = 0.10 $\frac{3}{20}$ = 0.15

What fraction is equivalent to 0.55? 0.75?

Make up other problems. Post them on the bulletin board for your classmates to solve.

If you walk 500 m around this building, where will you end up?

16 m
20 m
20 m
50 m
30 m
Start → 36 m

Comparing Ages of Inventions

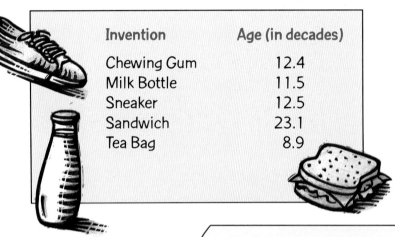

Invention	Age (in decades)
Chewing Gum	12.4
Milk Bottle	11.5
Sneaker	12.5
Sandwich	23.1
Tea Bag	8.9

Which invention is older — chewing gum or the tea bag?

Megan is using a number line.

Why do numbers farther to the right indicate greater age?

Tea Bag   Chewing Gum

0 1 2 3 4 5 6 7 8 9 10 11 12 13 14

Decades

12.4 is farther to the right than 8.9

so 12.4 > 8.9

Ken is changing decades to years. How many years is a decade?

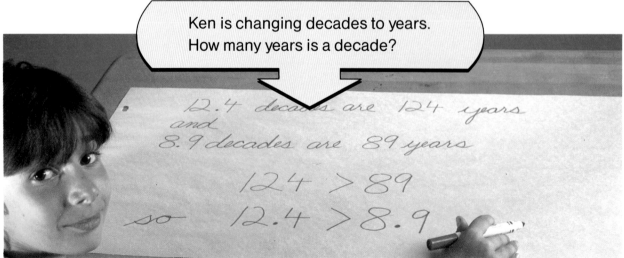

12.4 decades are 124 years
and
8.9 decades are 89 years

124 > 89

so   12.4 > 8.9

Ann is comparing the whole numbers.

$12 > 8$
so $12.4 > 8.9$

How did you decide which was older?
Whose method would not work to compare the ages of chewing gum and the sneaker?
How might that student compare those ages?

Work with a partner.

1. Show all the inventions from the previous page on a number line.
   Write 3 decimal comparisons about their ages.

2. Order these inventions from most recent to oldest.
   Write 3 decimal comparisons about them.

Invention	Age (in decades)
Chocolate Chip Cookie	6.3
Roller Skates	23.3
Television	6.7
Tin Can	18.1

3. How many years is a century?
   Show the ages of the inventions above in centuries.
   Write 3 decimal comparisons using the century ages.

4. How many decades old is each invention?

```
                                           Drinking
              Color Film        Zipper     Straw   Telephone
        |ılıılıılıılıılıılıılıılıılıılıılıılıılıılıılıılıılıılıılıılıılıılıılıılıılıılıılıılı|→
        0   1   2   3   4   5   6   7   8   9   10  11  12  13  14
        Decades
```

5. Show the ages in the number line in centuries.
   Write 3 decimal comparisons.

6. Describe other situations where you compare decimals.

55

A square pyramid is placed on each face of a cube. How many faces, edges, and vertices does the new shape have?

Comparing ingredients

Ordering fractions in right

Ordering fractions

Many recipes use fractions.

Yogurt Sauce

$\frac{3}{4}$ cup	yogurt	185 mL
$\frac{1}{4}$ cup	sugar	60 mL
$\frac{1}{8}$ cup	orange juice	30 mL
$\frac{1}{4}$ teaspoon	lemon juice	1 mL

Measure each pair to decide which is the greater amount. Then decide how you can tell by just comparing the numbers.

1. $\frac{1}{2}$ cup butter
   $\frac{1}{4}$ cup sugar

2. $\frac{1}{4}$ cup water
   $\frac{3}{4}$ cup flour

3. $\frac{1}{3}$ cup coconut
   $\frac{1}{2}$ cup pecans

4. $\frac{3}{8}$ cup oil
   $\frac{3}{4}$ cup sugar

Work in a group. **Use measuring cups.**

Gumdrop Nut Bread

$\frac{2}{3}$ cup sugar

$\frac{1}{3}$ cup oil

$\frac{1}{2}$ cup walnut pieces

$\frac{3}{4}$ cup gumdrops

3 cups flour

1 cup milk

$\frac{1}{4}$ teaspoon salt

$\frac{1}{2}$ teaspoon vanilla

5. Tell how to use the numbers to decide which amount is greater.
   - flour or milk
   - sugar or oil
   - oil or walnut pieces

Can you look at just the fractions for vanilla and oil to decide which amount is greater? Explain.

$\frac{1}{2} = \boxed{\frac{2}{4}}$ and $\frac{2}{4} < \frac{3}{4}$ so

6. Fred is comparing walnut pieces and gumdrops.

Which is the greater amount? Explain what he is doing and why. Use his method to compare

$\frac{2}{3}$ and $\frac{5}{6}$ $\frac{2}{3}$ and $\frac{3}{4}$

7. Myra is comparing oil and gumdrops. Explain what she is doing and why. Compare these ingredients using Fred's method from Problem 6. Whose method do you like better? Why? How can you compare these ingredients another way?

$\frac{1}{3} = \frac{3}{9}$ and

$\frac{3}{9} < \frac{3}{4}$ because

9ths are smaller than 4ths

so $\frac{1}{3} < \frac{3}{4}$

8. Order the amounts of gumdrop nut bread ingredients from greatest to least. Describe how you did it.

9. Order the amounts of these ingredients from least to greatest. Tell how you did it.

$\frac{1}{3}$ cup oil

$\frac{1}{4}$ cup raisins

$\frac{2}{3}$ cup nuts

$\frac{3}{4}$ cup sugar

$\frac{3}{8}$ cup coconut

10. Why do measurements like $\frac{3}{6}$ cup and $\frac{6}{8}$ cup usually not appear in recipes?

STRING LENGTHS

By estimating, cut two pieces of string so that one is about 0.22 m longer than the other.
Then measure. How accurate were you?

DIFFERENT WAYS

Try to find at least 6 ways to use 1, 2, 3, and 4 to make this statement true.

SHARING THE EARTH

Look at an atlas. Which decimal describes the amount of the Earth taken by each land mass?

  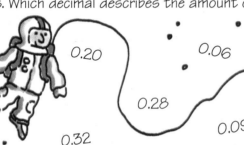

Africa
Antartica
Eurasia
Australasia
The Americas

0.20

0.06

0.28

0.32

0.09

COMPARING FRACTIONS

In $\frac{3}{4}$, $\frac{5}{6}$, and $\frac{7}{8}$, 5 is between 3 and 7, and 6 is between 4 and 8.
Is $\frac{5}{6}$ between $\frac{3}{4}$ and $\frac{7}{8}$?

Is the second fraction between the first and the third?

- $\frac{1}{4}$, $\frac{2}{8}$, and $\frac{3}{10}$?
- $\frac{1}{3}$, $\frac{2}{8}$, and $\frac{3}{10}$?

ZERO TO FOUR

Show 4 ways to use each of the digits from 1 to 4 to make this statement true.

$$0.\boxed{?}\boxed{?} > 0.\boxed{?}\boxed{?}$$

Make up other problems. Post them on the bulletin board for your classmates to solve.

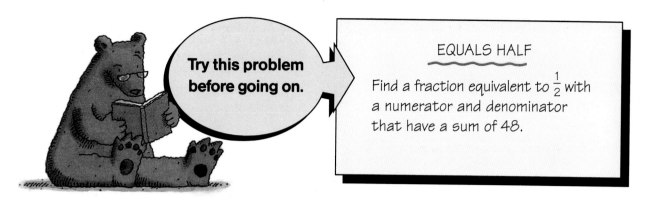

Try this problem before going on.

EQUALS HALF

Find a fraction equivalent to $\frac{1}{2}$ with a numerator and denominator that have a sum of 48.

Veronica's group solved the problem by guessing and testing.

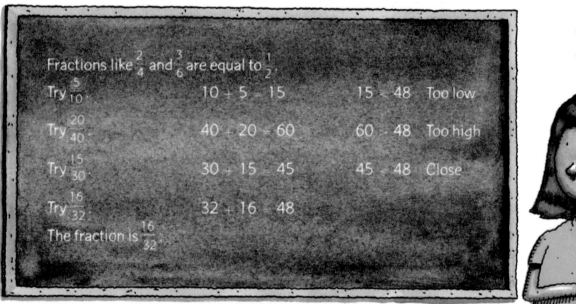

Fractions like $\frac{2}{4}$ and $\frac{3}{6}$ are equal to $\frac{1}{2}$.

Try $\frac{5}{10}$.   10 + 5 = 15   15 < 48   Too low

Try $\frac{20}{40}$.   40 + 20 = 60   60 > 48   Too high

Try $\frac{15}{30}$.   30 + 15 = 45   45 < 48   Close

Try $\frac{16}{32}$.   32 + 16 = 48

The fraction is $\frac{16}{32}$.

What if the fraction is to be equivalent to $\frac{1}{3}$?

Work in a group.

Solve these problems by guessing and testing.

SUM OF 15

Create a number so that
- the sum of its digits is 15
- the hundredths digit is greater than 5
- one digit is 3 greater than another
- the number is greater than 0.85

0.$\boxed{?}\boxed{?}$

GEOBOARD FRACTIONS

A shape that touches 4 pegs is $\frac{1}{6}$ of another shape that touches 10 pegs. What do the shapes look like?

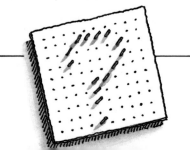

GREATER THAN

Find a rule that relates the denominators of these fractions to make this statement true.

$$\frac{3}{\boxed{?}} > \frac{6}{\boxed{?}}$$

Hint: First try $\frac{3}{\boxed{?}} = \frac{6}{\boxed{?}}$

59

1. Use hundredths grids to show

    0.15   0.20   0.24

2. Show each statement using models.

$\frac{1}{2} = 0.5$ $0.25 < 0.5$ $\frac{2}{3} < \frac{3}{4}$

$3.20 = 3.2$ $\frac{3}{4} > \frac{2}{5}$ $\frac{2}{3} = \frac{6}{9}$

3. Locate each on a number line.

    2.3   1.87 $\frac{3}{5}$ $\frac{7}{10}$

4. Describe each length as part of a metre.

    4 cm   58 cm   3 dm   6.2 dm

Solve these problems.

5. This centipede is wearing boots on 72 of its 100 feet. Describe the portion of feet wearing boots using a decimal.

6. Patrick is 1.25 m tall. How tall is he in centimetres? decimetres?

7. Who is the tallest? shortest? Who are closest in height?

Justin	Mabel	Anthony	Charlene	Bill
1.29 m	1.19 m	1.42 m	1.24 m	1.32 m

8. Write 2 equivalent fractions for each fraction.

    $\frac{1}{2}$ $\frac{3}{4}$ $\frac{2}{5}$ $\frac{5}{6}$ $\frac{4}{7}$

Playing Games for Practice

Play these games in pairs.

Dicey Fractions

- Toss a die twice.
- Make a fraction using the smaller number tossed as the numerator and the larger number as the denominator.
- Score 3 points if your fraction is equal to 1
  - 2 points if it is equal to 0.5
  - 1 point if it is between 0.5 and 1
  - 0 points if it is less than 0.5
- Take turns.
- The winner is the first player to reach 15 points.

Example

$\frac{2}{5} = \frac{4}{10} = 0.4$ and $0.4 < 0.5$ no points

Decimal Show Down

- Shuffle and deal all the cards face down.
- Both players turn over the top card in their piles.
- The player with the greater decimal takes both cards.
- If the decimals are equal, both players turn over another card. The player with the greater decimal takes all 4 cards.
- Play until one player has no cards left.

Example

$0.40 > 0.35$

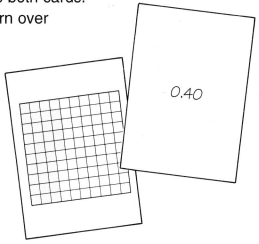

0.40

Variation: The player with the lesser decimal takes both cards.

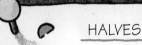

HALVES

How many fractions equivalent to $\frac{1}{2}$ are there with a 1-digit denomimator? a 2-digit denominator?

FOURS

What fraction of the numbers from 1 to 100 have a 4 in them? Express this as a decimal.

NAMING ODD SHAPES

What decimal is ◿ if ▢ is 1? if ▭ is 1?

What shape is 1 if this shape is 0.5?

REARRANGING DIGITS

Rearrange the digits of this number to make a number that is less than it.

How many numbers can you find?

SHARING A HEXAGON

Find a way to cut the hexagonal cake to share it equally among 5 people.

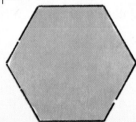

Make up other problems. Post them on the bulletin board for your classmates to solve.

1. Show 0.43 using two different models.

2. Explain why each piece is one-sixth.

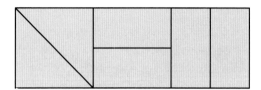

3. Use any digits to make this statement true.

   ? . ? > ? . ? ?

4. What happens to the size of a fraction when you
   • double both the numerator and the denominator?
   • triple the numerator and double the denominator?
   • double the numerator and triple the denominator?

5. Which is greater —
   the fraction of faces of a triangular prism that are triangles   or
   the fraction of faces of a hexagonal prism that are hexagons?

 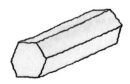

6. What are four other names for 0.25?

7. Who is right?

   This is 3 and 24 hundredths.

   This is 3 and 2 tenths, 4 hundredths.

   3.24

8. Show why $\frac{3}{5}$ is another name for $\frac{6}{10}$.
   What would be another name for $\frac{30}{50}$?

9. Change $\frac{1}{4}$ and $\frac{2}{5}$ to decimals.

   Is it easier to compare them as fractions or as decimals? Tell why.

Thinking Back

Tell a friend how you can use a number line to compare fractions and decimals.

0.23 is a lot bigger than 0.8.

Is Carlos right or wrong? Explain.

Zeros aren't needed after the decimal point to show decimals because 0.2 = 0.20.

Tell Sophie why she's not quite right.

Tell as many things about $\frac{1}{6}$ as you can.

APPLES 2 for 0.99¢

What is wrong with the sign? How would you correct it?

What questions do you still have about fractions and decimals?

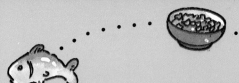

UNIT
4

Investigating Nutrition and Health

NUTRITION INFORMATION APPORT NUTRITIONNEL		
Per 40 g serving cereal (175 mL, ¾ cup) Par ration de 40 g de céréale (175 mL, ¾ tasse)	Per 40 g serving cereal with 125 mL Partly Skimmed Milk (2%) Par ration de 40 g de céréale avec 125 mL de lait partiellement écrémé (2,0 %)	
ENERGY	130Cal	195Cal	ÉNERGIE
	540kJ	810kJ	
PROTEIN	3.0g	7.3g	PROTÉINES
FAT	0.4g	2.9g	MATIÈRES GRASSES
CARBOHYDRATE	32g	38g	GLUCIDES
SUGARS*	11g	18g	*SUCRES
STARCH	16g	16g	AMIDON
DIETARY FIBRE	4.6g	4.6g	FIBRES ALIMENTAIRES
SODIUM	235mg	300mg	SODIUM
POTASSIUM	240mg	440mg	POTASSIUM

NUTRITION INFORMATION NUTRITIONNELLE per 250 mL serving (1 cup) par portion de 250 mL (1 tasse)		
Energy / Énergie	108	Cal
	450	kJ
Protein / Protéines	8.5	g
Fat / Matières grasses	2.7	g
Carbohydrate / Glucides	12	g
% RECOMMENDED DAILY INTAKE % de L'APPORT QUOTIDIEN RECOMMANDÉ		
Vitamin / Vitamine A		11%
Vitamin / Vitamine D		44%
Calcium		29%

About how many servings of milk are in the milk carton?

How can you tell that about one quarter of the cereal is sugar?

What other problems can you create using this information?

Collect empty food packages and read the labels. What numbers and measurements can you find?

65

WHAT Is in Fast Food?

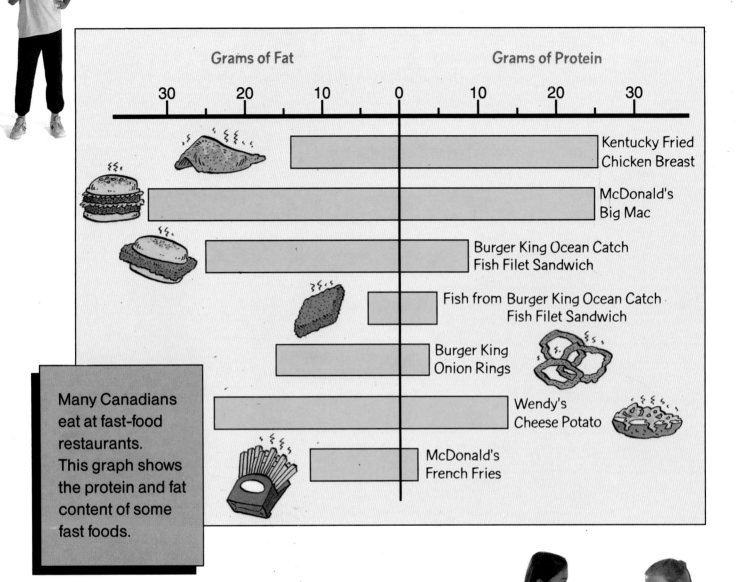

Many Canadians eat at fast-food restaurants. This graph shows the protein and fat content of some fast foods.

Grams of Fat | **Grams of Protein**

30 20 10 0 10 20 30

- Kentucky Fried Chicken Breast
- McDonald's Big Mac
- Burger King Ocean Catch Fish Filet Sandwich
- Fish from Burger King Ocean Catch Fish Filet Sandwich
- Burger King Onion Rings
- Wendy's Cheese Potato
- McDonald's French Fries

Use the graph.

1. Which foods contain more fat than protein?

2. Which food contains the most fat? the least?

3. Which food contains the most protein? the least?

4. Compare the two potato foods.
   What might explain the differences in fat and protein content?

5. Tell how you know that the average amount of fat in these foods is greater than 10 g and less than 30 g.
   What do you think the average amount of fat is?

66

Work in a group.

6. About how much protein do you need each day? Which foods in the graph would provide one third or more of this daily requirement?

7. In the graph, the fish in a Fish Filet Sandwich has a mass of about 100 g. The same mass of fish when cooked in a microwave has about 1.0 g of fat and 19.0 g of protein.
How would a bar graph of this look different from the graph for the fish in the Fish Filet Sandwich?

The Food We Eat

Protein is essential for muscle and tissue growth, repair, and maintenance. About 0.15 of our energy should come from protein. We need about 40 g each day. Good sources of protein are meats, beans, and dairy products.

We need to eat fat for healthy skin, steady body temperature, and reserve energy. Fat is necessary for absorbing certain vitamins and is a source of essential nutrients. Most Canadians eat too much fat. We get about 0.40 of our energy from fat and we should get no more than 0.30.

8. This chart shows the amount of protein and fat in some other fast foods.

Food	Grams of Protein	Grams of Fat
Dairy Queen Hounder	16.0	36.0
Taco Bell Taco	10.0	11.0
Pizza Hut Pepperoni Pan Pizza	29.0	22.0
Wendy's Garden Salad	7.0	5.0

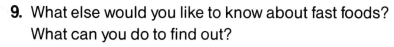
Make a bar graph to display this information.

9. What else would you like to know about fast foods? What can you do to find out?

67

How Should We Display Data?

Examine the fast food graph on page 66.

1. Which of the following comparisons is the most difficult? Explain.
   - comparing the fat content of McDonald's French fries with a Big Mac
   - comparing the protein content of McDonald's French fries and a Big Mac
   - comparing the fat and protein content of a Big Mac

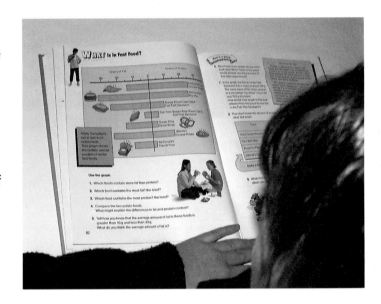

The students in Karen's class displayed the same data to make it easier to compare the fat and protein content of each food.

Karen made a chart.

Product	Grams of Fat (g)	Grams of Protein (g)
Kentucky Fried Chicken Breast	14	25
McDonald's Big Mac	33	24
Burger King Ocean Catch Sandwich	25	8
Burger King Onion Rings	18	3
Wendy's Cheese Potato	24	13
McDonald's French Fries	12	2

Trevor made a double bar graph.

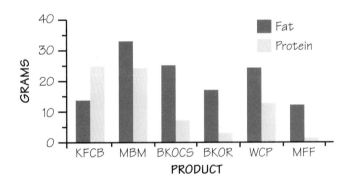

2. What other comparisons can you make with the chart and graph?

3. The protein and fat contents of some hamburgers are very similar. How would you display data to compare each hamburger's fat and protein content? Explain.

4. Make a double bar graph for the data in Problem 8 on page 67.

5. Why might you choose a chart rather than a graph to compare data that ranges from 3 g to 2 kg?

How Can We Group Data?

Pauline's class investigated the question "What foods are favorite?"

Pauline improved the question to "What are favorite desserts?" and decided to use these groupings:

- fresh fruit
- frozen treats
- pies
- cookies
- puddings
- other

1. What grouping do you think doughnuts belong to? cake? Jello?

2. What food would you investigate? What groupings would you use?

Pauline improved the question more to "What are favorite desserts among children ages 3 to 11?"

3. What is the total population of her investigation?

Pauline improved the question again to "Does age affect children's dessert choices?" To compare different ages, she used these groups:

- ages 3 to 5
- ages 6 to 8
- ages 9 to 11

4. Why do you think she chose these age groups? What might you use?

5. What sample should she use? How might she collect the data?

Work in a group.

6. Design an investigation for your food choice from Problem 2.

   Determine
   - groupings for your food type
   - the total population and what groups you will compare
   - what sample you would use
   - how to collect the data

7. Why is it a good idea to wait until the data is collected before deciding on how to display it?

69

WHERE Is the Sugar?

Sugar and Fibre Content of Ten Breakfast Cereals

Cereal	Grams of sugar per 30 g serving	Grams of fibre per 30 g serving	Package size in grams
Corn Flakes	2.3	0.8	400
Honey Nut Corn Flakes	9.2	0.8	525
Bran Flakes	3.3	4.4	475
Froot Loops	14.0	0.5	275
Grape Nuts	2.1	3.6	375
Shreddies	4.7	2.7	675
Marshmallow Alpha-Bits	15.0	0.8	400
Rice Krispies	2.9	0.3	350
Sugar Crisp	13.0	1.2	400
All Bran	5.3	10.0	575

Work in a group.

Use the chart.

1. Order the cereals from the greatest to least amount of sugar per serving.

2. Which cereals are about half sugar? For each cereal, about how many spoonfuls of sugar are in one serving?

3. Which cereals are about one third sugar? less than one tenth sugar?

5 g

4. The recommended daily intake of fibre is 25 to 30 g. Which cereals provide about one third of your daily fibre in each serving? more than one tenth?

5. About how many servings of Froot Loops would you need to eat to provide one third of your daily fibre?

6. About how many servings of cereal are in the package with the greatest mass? the least mass?

7. Can you tell from the names of the cereals which ones contain the greatest amounts of sugar? Explain.

8. How do you know that All Bran cereal is not all bran?

9. Each decimal describes the portion of a cereal that is sugar. Make up a name that you think best describes the sweetness of each cereal.

0.01   0.50   0.95

10. What are the fibre and sugar contents of your favorite cereal? Can you find other cereals that contain more fibre and less sugar?

Did You Know...?

Many cans of soft drinks contain from about 40 mL to 50 mL of sugar.

▶ About how many spoonfuls of sugar are in each can? If you drink one can a day, about how many cans of sugar will you drink each week?

? I Wonder... ?

Two Scoops

About how many raisins are in each scoop? What could you do to find out? Do you think the scoops are the same size for a 60 g package?

Meaty Peanuts

100 g of peanuts contain about 49 g of fat and about 24 g of protein. Estimate the amount of fat and protein in a 1 kg container of natural peanut butter.
Explain why peanuts are grouped with meats rather than fruits and vegetable

Healthy Eating

Conduct a survey to find out which of the food groups in Canada's Food Guide people prefer. What would your survey question be? How would you group your data? How might you display it?

Disappearing Gum

Find the mass of 5 Chiclets in a small cup. Cover the Chiclets with hot water and leave them for a few hours. Carefully drain the water out so the gum stays in. Let the cup and gum dry overnight.
Find the mass of the cup and Chiclets again.
How can you explain what you saw and measured?

Comparing Potatoes

How many servings of french fries can you make from an average potato? How much would these french fries cost at a fast-food restaurant? Compare this to the cost of the potato.

Make up your OWN investigation. Then post it on the bulletin board for others to try.

72

Thinking Back

What part of the chicken egg do you think is missing from the imitation egg product? Use this information to help you explain.

Poached Egg

2.8 g protein
5.1 g fat

Egg Substitute

6.3 g protein
0 g fat

3.5 g protein
0 g fat

Examine numbers and measurement units shown on food packages. Tell what you know about these numbers and units.

Tell what you notice about this chart. Investigate why calcium is an important nutrient. What foods and drinks contain calcium? How would you display this data in a graph? Why?

Recommended Daily Amounts of Calcium		
Age (years)	Females (mg per day)	Males (mg per day)
under 4	500	500
4-6	600	600
7-9	700	700
10-12	1000	900
13-15	800	1100
16-18	700	900
19-49	700	800
over 50	800	800

Source: Health and Welfare Canada

Conduct a survey of jam preferences. How would you group your data? display your data? Write about what you found out.

What else would you like to know about nutrition and health? Describe what you would do to find out.

Extending

◀ Tell how 4 friends can share 8 sandwiches.
What fraction of the 8 sandwiches will each get?

▼ Complete each division.

$3\overline{)4}$ $3\overline{)7}$ $3\overline{)10}$ $3\overline{)13}$ $3\overline{)16}$

What patterns do you notice? What division would you write next?

▼ Ravi is dividing 240 by 6.

What can he do next?

$240 \div 3 = 80$

Division

▲ Show how to fold a 100 cm tape to find these parts.

$\frac{1}{2}$ of 100 $\frac{1}{4}$ of 100

◀ A man roller-skated 1488 km in just over 9 days. How can these calculations help you estimate how far he skated each day?

$9 \times 100 = 900$

$9 \times 200 = 1800$

▼ Use one of these facts in a division problem.

365 days in 1 year
500 sheets in a package
210 staples in a strip
250 mL in a carton

Describe two ways to find how much time has passed between **9:45 AM** and **2:40 PM**

Displaying Collections

Stefan has 3 shelves on which to display 16 model planes.

Can he display them with an equal number on each shelf? Explain. How many planes will be on each shelf?

Jackie is displaying 16 model planes with 3 on each shelf.

How many shelves will she use to display them? Why?

Explain each number in Stefan's division sentence.

16 ÷ 3 = 5 + R1

dividend **divisor** **quotient** **remainder**

Explain each number in Jackie's division sentence.

16 ÷ 3 = 5 + R1

How are the two division methods different? the same?

76

Work with a partner.

Model each solution by sharing or making equal groups of counters.

1. Which number of planes can be displayed with the same number of them on each of Stefan's 3 shelves?

   18   24   28   37

   How many will be on each shelf?

2. How many shelves will Jackie use to display each number of planes with 3 on each shelf?

   17   22   33   39

3. Make up a division problem about planes and 3 shelves using this division sentence.

   $23 \div 3 = 7 + R2$

4. Make up a division problem about planes with 3 on each shelf using this division sentence.

   $$\begin{array}{r} 9 + R2 \\ 3\overline{)29} \end{array}$$

---

5. Six hockey cards can be displayed on one page.
   How many pages are needed to display 37 cards? 42 cards? 57 cards? Write a division sentence for each.

6. A hockey card display has between 30 and 40 cards. If each page has exactly 6 cards, how many cards are displayed?

---

7. Stamps are displayed with the same number on a page. There are no stamps left over when either 6 or 8 pages are used. How many stamps might be displayed?

8. Stamps are displayed with the same number on a page. There is 1 stamp left over when 3, 4, or 5 pages are used. How many stamps might be displayed?

9. Make up a division problem about something that people like to display in books or on shelves.

Double your age in years. Then multiply the result by 5. Remove the ones digit. What do you notice? Why did this happen?

Celebrating Fraction Birthdays

Daniel sent this invitation.

My sister Katie is 6 months old. Please come to her half-birthday party on Sunday afternoon at 3 o'clock. And bring half a present.

Daniel

P.S. You have to tell a whole story about the half present.

from *The Half-Birthday Party* by Charlotte Pomerantz

What is half of this present?

All of these show that half of 20 rings is 10.

$\frac{1}{2}$ of 20 = 10   20 ÷ 2 = 10 $2\overline{)20}^{10}$

Which way would you write it? Why?

Work in a group.

Model using fraction mats and counters. Write a sentence with a fraction and a division sentence when appropriate.

1. What is one half of each present? What is one fourth? one third?

78

2. A present is 100 blocks. What would be one-half of a present? What would be a one-fourth present?

3. Twelve farm animals are a present for a birthday. What would be the present for a one-third birthday?

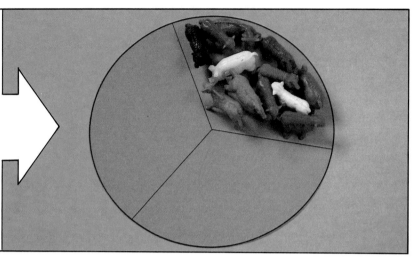

4. Eight picture books are a present for a one-year birthday. What would be the present for a $\frac{1}{2}$ year birthday?

5. Fifteen shapes are a present for a birthday. What would be the present for a $\frac{1}{3}$ birthday?

• a $\frac{2}{3}$ birthday?

6. A present for a one-half birthday is 100 building pieces and a one-year birthday is 200 building pieces. What would be the present for a one-fourth birthday?

7.

What is about half of this present?

269 CONNECTING SHAPES

8. Which would you choose to make a present for a two-thirds birthday? Explain.

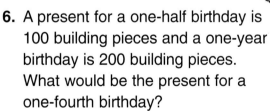

24 BLOCKS   20 BLOCKS

9. What present would you bring to a fraction birthday party? Write a story about it. Tell how you determined how much to bring.

Joan drove 80 km in 1 h. For the first 30 min, she drove at a speed of 60 km/h. What was her speed for the rest of the hour?

Placing Racing Flags

Five flags are equally spaced around the perimeter of a 200 cm race track.
How far apart are the flags?

Lise is using the fact that $20 \div 5 = 4$.

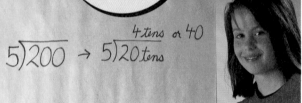

$5\overline{)200} \rightarrow 5\overline{)20 \text{ tens}}$ 4 tens or 40

Use a different way to find how far apart the flags are.
How would the answer change if the track was 400 cm long?

Work in a group.   **Use facts you know.**

1. Find the distance between each pair of flags.
   Write each division sentence.

   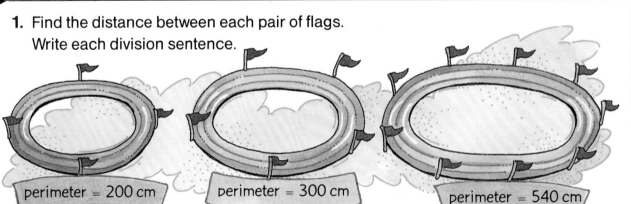

   perimeter = 200 cm   perimeter = 300 cm   perimeter = 540 cm

2. Make up and solve a racing flag problem for each division.

   $800 \div 2$ $3\overline{)900}$ $120 \div 4$

80

3. Show how the fact 45 ÷ 5 = 9 can help you find the distance between each pair of flags.

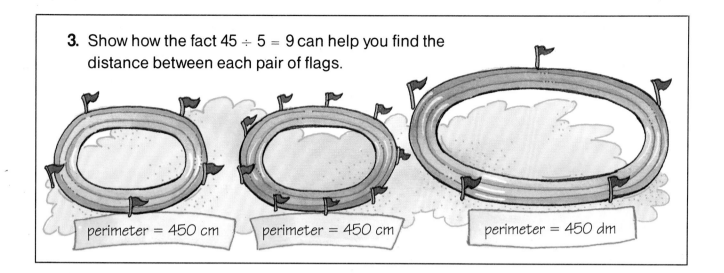

perimeter = 450 cm   perimeter = 450 cm   perimeter = 450 dm

4. Copy and complete the table. What patterns do you notice?

Perimeter in centimetres	30	300
Number of flags	5	5
Distance between flags	?	?

5. Use digits that will make a true statement. Make up a racing flag problem for it.

$$\boxed{?}\,0$$
$$\boxed{?}\,)\,\overline{\boxed{?}\,\boxed{?}\,0}$$

6. Find the distance between the flags on the first two tracks. Then show how those answers can be used to find the distance between the flags on the last track.

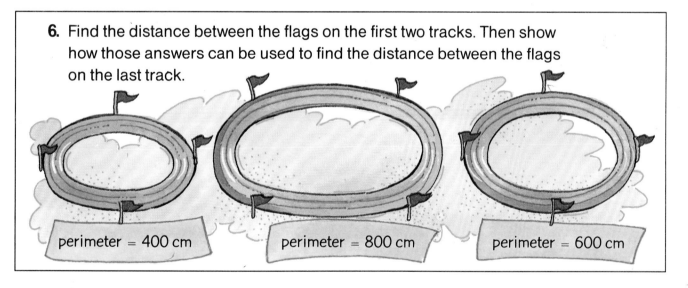

perimeter = 400 cm   perimeter = 800 cm   perimeter = 600 cm

7. How many centimetres are between each pair of flags on these race tracks?

- 6 flags equally spaced around a 3 m track
- 12 flags equally spaced around a 6 m track

8. Which division is easiest for you to do? Explain. Make up a racing flag problem for it.

$7\,)\,\overline{96}$ $3\,)\,\overline{600}$ $2\,)\,\overline{479}$

81

Each day Karen painted twice as much
of a long fence as she did the day before.
It took her 30 days to paint the entire fence.
After how many days was the fence half painted?

Dividing Animal Groups

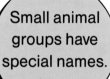

Small animal groups have special names.

a band of gorillas
a brood of chicks
a cloud of gnats
a clowder of cats
a colony of ants
a crash of rhinoceroses
a cry of hounds
a drift of swine
a flock of birds

a gaggle of geese
a gang of elks
a knot of toads
a mob of kangaroos
a murder of crows
a pod of whales
a sloth of bears
a troop of monkeys
a yoke of oxen

Try this problem.

A mob of 271 kangaroos split up into 4 almost equal groups. Each group hopped in a different direction. About how many kangaroos hopped in each direction?

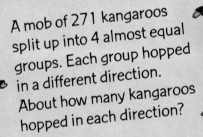

Ravi used a division fact he knew.

Linda used a different division fact.

$4)\overline{271}$ is about $4)\overline{280}$

$\dfrac{7\text{ tens} \text{ or } 70}{4)\overline{28}\text{ tens}}$

$4)\overline{271}$ is about $4)\overline{240}$

$\dfrac{6\text{ tens} \text{ or } 60}{4)\overline{24}\text{ tens}}$

How could you use both estimates to find a better estimate?

82

**Use facts you know to help you estimate.
Explain how you estimated.**

1. About half of a knot of 191 toads sat on a log. About how many toads were not sitting on the log?

2. A troop of 339 monkeys split up and swung in almost equal numbers from 6 trees. About how many monkeys swung from each tree?

3. 235 rhinoceroses came together from 8 approximately equal crashes. About how many rhinoceroses were in each crash?

**Explain how each pair of calculations can help you solve the problem.
Then make up another problem that each pair could help you solve.**

4. A colony of 378 ants built 5 nests. About how many ants can live in each nest?

$$\begin{array}{r} 70 \\ 5\overline{)350} \end{array} \qquad \begin{array}{r} 80 \\ 5\overline{)400} \end{array}$$

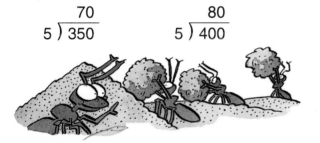

5. A gaggle of geese migrated 300 km in 1 week. About how far did they travel each day?

$$\begin{array}{r} 40 \\ \times\,7 \\ \hline 280 \end{array} \qquad \begin{array}{r} 50 \\ \times\,7 \\ \hline 350 \end{array}$$

Use a fact you know to estimate. How can you get a closer estimate?

6. A murder of crows flew to 463 farms in 6 weeks. About how many farms did they fly to each week?

Make up division estimating problems for another group to solve.

7. Use any animal group name listed.

8. Use an animal group name that is not listed.

83

Draw the shape of the cross section when a cheese tube is cut like this.

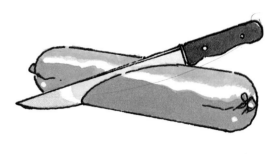

Delivering Flyers

Four friends agreed to share the delivery of 135 flyers as equally as possible.

How many flyers should each deliver?

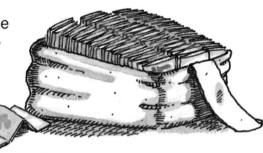

Angela renamed the dividend.

$$4\overline{)135} \rightarrow 4\overline{)\,\overset{30 + 3 + R3}{120 + 12 + 3}}$$

Why did she choose these numbers? Finish her work.

Leon renamed the dividend differently.

$$4\overline{)135} \rightarrow 4\overline{)\,\overset{20 + 10 + 3 + R3}{80 + 40 + 12 + 3}}$$

Explain why he chose these numbers. Finish his work.

Show another way to divide 135 by 4 by renaming the dividend.

Work in a group.

Rename the dividends with numbers you can divide easily by the divisors.

1. Show how each number of friends can deliver 205 flyers as equally as possible.

   3   5   9

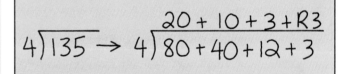

84

2. Rename 260 flyers two different ways to show how they can be delivered equally by 5 friends.

3. Which renaming would you use to divide 345 flyers by 4? Explain.

$$4 \overline{)\,300 + 40 + 4 + 1}$$

$$4 \overline{)\,200 + 100 + 44 + 1}$$

$$4 \overline{)\,320 + 24 + 1}$$

4. Rename the number of flyers to help you divide each by 6. Which did you find easiest to divide? Explain.

612   558   212   672

5. Use any digit so that the flyers can be divided equally.

⬚02 flyers delivered by 2

832 flyers delivered by ⬚

54⬚ flyers delivered by 5

6. Find a 3-digit number of flyers that can be divided equally among 2, 3, or 4 friends. What is the least 3-digit number that works? the greatest?

7. Five friends are delivering 800 flyers altogether. They are being paid 4¢ for each flyer. How much money should each receive? How long would it take the friends to deliver the flyers?

How many times would you have to write your first name to have more than 100 letters?

Sharing the Booty

Each of 6 salvage hunters receives an equal share of 96 boots.

What division does this suggest?

Philip found each boat's share.

Then he found each individual's share.

Explain why this method divides the boots into 6 equal shares.

Use only halves, thirds, and fifths mats.

1. Find the share of each item for 6 salvage hunters.

   72 tires   132 bottles
   150 fishing lures

2. Show how 120 boots can be shared equally among each number of salvage hunters.

   4   8   6   10   12

3. Which number of shares cannot be found using the fraction mats you have? Explain.

   7   8   9   10   11

4. Share 100 bottles among 10 salvage hunters.
   For what other number of salvage hunters could you use the same two mats to find equal shares of 100 bottles?

86

Take Your Pick

CALCULATOR PATTERN

Complete each division.
What is the next division?
What patterns do you notice?
Make up a similar pattern
starting with a different division.

$31 \div 5$

$62 \div 5$

$124 \div 5$

$248 \div 5$

$496 \div 5$

SOUTHPAWS

There is about 1 left-handed
person for every 10 right-handed
people.
Estimate the number of
left-handed people in

* your class

* your school

* your community

SHARING PHONE LISTS

A list of numbers to be phoned was divided equally between 2 students.
Each of those students divided their lists equally among 3 other students.
Each of those students divided their lists equally among 5 other students.
What might have been the number of phone numbers on the list?

OOPS!

Keith was dividing 456 by 5 on his
calculator but pressed the wrong
button. He divided 466 instead.
How can he correct his mistake
without starting over?

PICKING DIGITS

How many pairs of digits can
you use so that the answer is a
whole number?

$6\boxed{?} \div \boxed{?}$

**Make up other problems. Post them
on the bulletin board for your
classmates to solve.**

111
333
555
777
+ 999

Rewrite this addition leaving out as many digits as necessary so that the sum is 1111.

F inding Prizes

Every 7th bottle cap shows a prize.
How many prizes are there in a shipment of 950 caps?

Lia is dividing 950 by 7 to find the number of prizes.

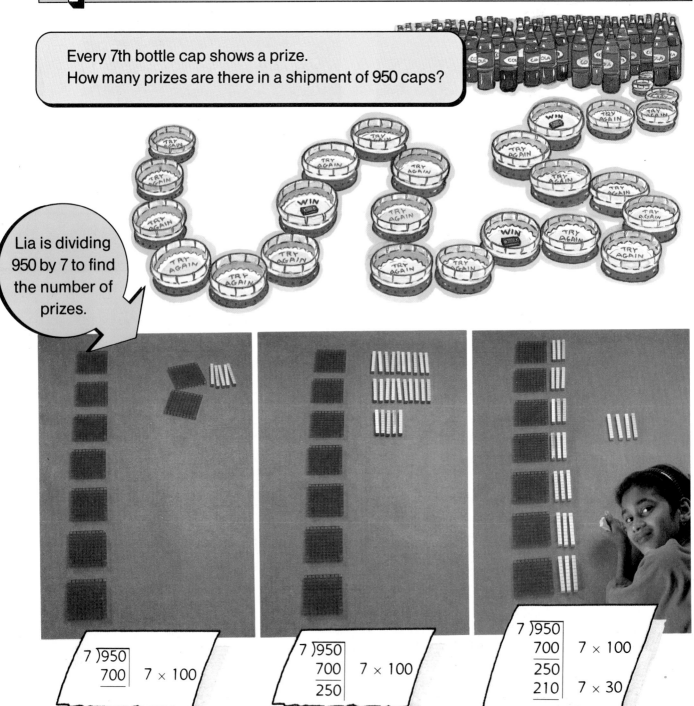

$$7 \overline{)950}$$
$700 \quad 7 \times 100$

$$7 \overline{)950}$$
$700 \quad 7 \times 100$
$\overline{250}$

$$7 \overline{)950}$$
$700 \quad 7 \times 100$
$\overline{250}$
$210 \quad 7 \times 30$

Finish her work. Check your answer by dividing another way.

Use base ten blocks. Check your answers by dividing another way or by multiplying.

1. How many prizes are there in a shipment of 264 bottles if a prize is shown under every second cap? third cap? fourth cap?

2. One cap in each carton shows a prize. How many prizes are there in a shipment of 750 bottles?

3. Prizes are under every fifth cap. Show how the multiplication fact
   120 × 5 = 600 can help you find the number of prizes in

   615 caps   585 caps

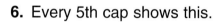

4. Prizes are shown under every eighth cap. How many prizes are there in a shipment of 896 bottles?

5. Every third cap shows a prize. Every eighth prize is double the value of the others.
   How many prizes are there in a shipment of 975 bottles?
   How many prizes are double the value of the others?

6. Every 5th cap shows this.

   How many caps show NEXT BOTTLE FREE in a shipment of 975 bottles?

7. Now try this one. Every 9th cap shows a prize. How many prizes are there in a shipment of 990 bottles?

8. Make up a division problem about prizes for another group to solve.

Dividing

There are lots of ways to calculate 268 ÷ 4.
Here are some. Can you think of any more?

1. You might rename 268 as a sum of numbers easily divided by 4.

$$\begin{array}{r} 60 + 7 = 67 \\ 4\overline{)240 + 28} \end{array}$$

268 ÷ 4 = 67

2. You could rename 268 as a difference of numbers easily divided by 4.

$$\begin{array}{r} 70 - 3 = 67 \\ 4\overline{)280 - 12} \end{array}$$

268 ÷ 4 = 67

3. You might divide 268 in half twice. Check using base ten blocks.

$\frac{1}{2}$ of 268 $\frac{1}{2}$ of 134

268 ÷ 2 = 134   134 ÷ 2 = 67

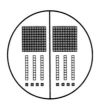   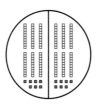

268 ÷ 4 = 67

4. You could multiply and subtract in steps.

$$\begin{array}{r} 4\overline{)268} \\ 200 \\ \hline 68 \\ 48 \\ \hline 20 \\ 20 \\ \hline 0 \end{array}$$

4×50

4×12

4×5
___
67

268 ÷ 4 = 67

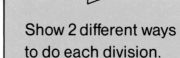

Work in a group.

Show 2 different ways to do each division.

1. 137 ÷ 3   **2.** 4$\overline{)96}$

3. 6$\overline{)288}$ **4.** 100 ÷ 4

5. 5$\overline{)275}$ **6.** 8$\overline{)699}$

Take Your Pick

DECIMAL REMAINDERS

Choose 5 odd numbers.
Use a calculator to divide each number by 2.
What do you notice about each answer?
Now divide each of your odd numbers by 4.
What do you notice now?

PLACING DIGITS

Place the digits 1, 3, 5, and 7 to make the
- greatest quotient
- least quotient

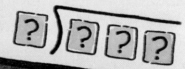

COUNTING SIT-UPS

Louis set a class record when he did 409 sit-ups in 8 min.
To achieve his record, about how many did he have to do each minute?

ANCIENT CAPACITY MEASURES

Many centuries ago, people used the following units to measure amounts of liquids

2 mouthfulls = 1 jigger
2 jiggers = 1 jack
2 jacks = 1 jill
2 jills = 1 cup

How many cups are needed to hold 256 mouthfulls?

Make up a similar problem for someone else to solve.

FEDERAL ELECTIONS

The federal government must hold an election at least every 5 years.
At least how many elections have been held since Canada was formed in 1867?
Explain why Canada had only 18 prime ministers by iys 125th birthday in 1992.

Make up other problems. Post them on the bulletin board for your classmates to solve.

Try this problem before going on.

MARBLES

Jerry has half as many marbles as Billy. Billy has one third as many as Harry. Harry has one quarter as many as Garry. How many marbles does each boy have if Garry has 240 marbles?

Cecilia's group solved the problem by working backwards.

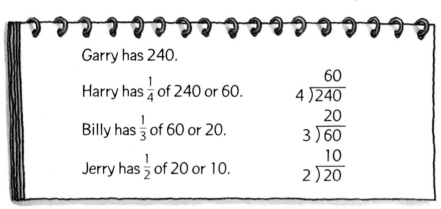

Garry has 240.

Harry has $\frac{1}{4}$ of 240 or 60.

$$4\overline{)240} \quad 60$$

Billy has $\frac{1}{3}$ of 60 or 20.

$$3\overline{)60} \quad 20$$

Jerry has $\frac{1}{2}$ of 20 or 10.

$$2\overline{)20} \quad 10$$

What if Garry had only 72 marbles?

Work with a partner.

Solve each problem by working backwards.

SHARING JELLY BEANS

Sally shared her jelly beans with Kelly and Millie. Each girl received an equal number with one left over. Then Kelly shared her jelly beans with Jenny. Each girl received an equal number with one left over. How many jelly beans did Sally start with if Jenny received 12?

WANDERING ANT

An ant walked 5 cm across this page, turned and walked down 6 cm, turned and walked across 5 cm. It ended up at the bottom left corner. Where could it have started?

EATING APPLES

An elephant ate half a basket of apples on Sunday. Then it ate half the remaining apples on Monday. Each day it ate half the remaining apples until on Saturday there was only one apple left to eat. How many apples were in the basket on Sunday?

Practising What You've Learned

Write a problem for each of these. Then solve.

1. 48 ÷ 3   **2.** 960 ÷ 8

3. 5$\overline{)120}$ **4.**

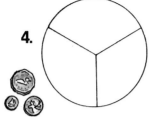

Solve problems 5 to 10. Indicate those that use division.

5. About how many days are there when one year is divided into 4 equal parts?

6. A restaurant uses 4 dozen eggs each day. How many eggs does it use in a week? in a month?

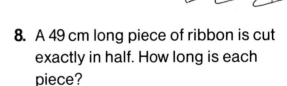

7. The sides of a hexagon are equal in length. The perimeter is 90 cm. What is the length of each side?

8. A 49 cm long piece of ribbon is cut exactly in half. How long is each piece?

9. Joanne bought 5 cassette tapes costing $2.98 each. Use a calculator to find how much change she will receive from a $20 bill.

10. Edward trades 128 pennies for nickels. How many nickels does he receive? How many more pennies does he need to receive another nickel?

11. Divide.

6$\overline{)216}$ 7$\overline{)343}$

8$\overline{)403}$ 9$\overline{)539}$

12. Jay's family drove 645 km in 3 days. How far did they drive each day?

Playing Games for Practice

Play each game in a group of 2, 3, or 4.

Divide and Conquer

- Remove the face cards and aces from a deck of playing cards.
- Shuffle the cards and place them face down in a pile.
- Turn over the top card.
- Place a counter on any unoccupied number on a 100 chart that can be divided evenly by the number on your card.
- Each player uses a different color of counters.
- Take turns until no unoccupied numbers can be divided evenly by the numbers on the cards.
- The player with the greatest number of counters on the chart is the winner.

Variation: The player having the greatest sum of the numbers under the counters is the winner.

Example

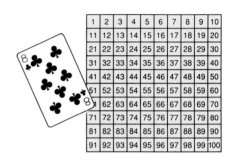

A counter could be placed on 32.
What other numbers are possible?

Rolling Remainders

- Roll one dice twice to get a 2-digit dividend using the digits in the order rolled.
- Roll the die again to get a 1-digit divisor.
- Divide and find the remainder.
- Place a counter on any unoccupied space showing a number equal to your remainder.
- Each player uses a different color of counters.
- Take turns until the board is covered with counters.
- The winner is the player with the greatest number of counters on the board.

Example

$$\begin{array}{r} 15\text{ R}1 \\ 3\overline{)46} \\ 30 \\ \hline 16 \\ 15 \\ \hline 1 \end{array}$$

Place a counter on 1.

0	1	0	1	2
0	1	2	3	0
1	2	3	4	0
1	2	3	4	5

Take Your Pick

SHRINKING AWAY

Suppose you find that each day you are half as tall as you were the day before. In how many days will you be shorter than your pencil? On what day will you be able to walk under the classroom door?

LEFTOVER DOLLARS

You get to keep any leftover $1 coins after sharing 100 of them equally among less than 9 young children. Among how many children would you prefer to share them? Why?

BLAST FROM THE PAST

Solve this problem given to students in 1869.

A school has 3 classrooms.
$\frac{1}{4}$ of the boys are in the first classroom.
$\frac{1}{4}$ of the boys are in the second.
20 boys are in the third.

How many boys are in each classroom?

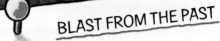

LEAP YEARS

Any year that can be divided evenly by 4 is a leap year, except century years, which must be divided evenly by 400. To find out if 1996 was a leap year, you can just divide 996 by 4.
How would you find out if the year 2026 was a leap year?

DIVIDING BY 7

Use a calculator to divide each number from 7 to 13 by 7. Record each decimal remainder. Describe any patterns you see. Predict the decimal remainders when numbers from 14 to 20 are divided by 7. Check your prediction by dividing.

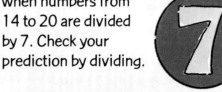

Make up other problems. Post them on the bulletin board for your classmates to solve.

1. Make up and solve a division problem for each situation.

2. Use two different non-zero digits that will allow you to divide in your head.

3. How does knowing 420 ÷ 6 help you find 432 ÷ 6?

4. Show how to use this fraction mat to share these crayons among 8 students.

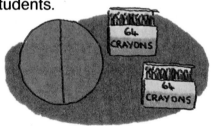

5. Use any number.

$\boxed{?} \times 2 \times 2 \times 2 \div 8 =$

Try other numbers. What happens? Explain why.

6. If you cut and tape squares of paper, how many nets of cubes can you make from a 10 × 10 grid?

7. Six friends shared a bag of apples. Each received 3 apples and there were 2 left over. How many apples were in the bag originally?

8. Without doing the actual calculations, decide which answer is closest to 50. Explain what you did.

$4 \overline{)\,348}$ $5 \overline{)\,259}$ $8 \overline{)\,486}$

9. What digits make this sentence true?

$\frac{1}{\boxed{?}}$ of 240 > 59

10. A 3-digit number is divided by 8 using a calculator. Which is a reasonable answer?

5.825   58.25   582.5

How would you explain to a friend how to correct this error?

$$6 \overline{)\overset{2}{120}}$$

How could you still solve sharing problems if division was banned?

Explain how division might be used to find how many pickets are needed for a fence.

How many cars are needed to take 18 students to the museum if 4 students travel in each car? Which answer makes the most sense? Tell why.

4 + R2

4

5

Which division would you rather do in your head? Why?

$$4 \overline{)200} \qquad 7 \overline{)169}$$

What questions do you still have about division?

▼ Which would you more likely measure the mass of in grams? in kilograms?

Name two other things you would measure in each unit.

Which unit would you want to use to measure the distance from your home to your school? Why?

centimetre   metre   kilometre

▼ What might the 10 cm describe?

▼ What containers have capacities between 5 L and 10 L?

BUILD A MODEL ROCKET

Use construction paper to make the body of the rocket. The body should be 10 cm

Measurement

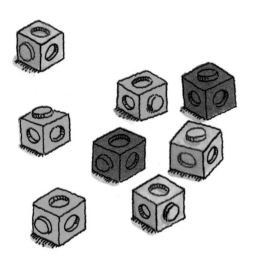

How many different prisms can you build with 7 cubes? 8 cubes? Tell what you notice.

For each colored square, what is the perimeter? the area?

Use grid paper. Draw a square where the number describing its perimeter is

- equal to the number describing its area
- greater than the number describing its area
- less than the number describing its area

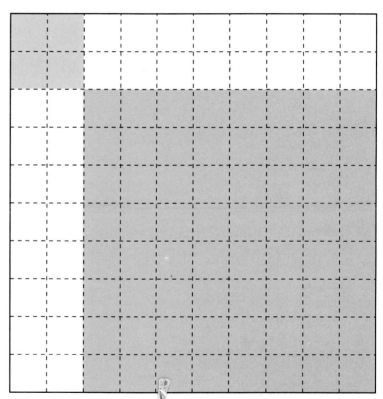

Which measurement— mass, volume, length, or width— is most useful to describe a pencil? Tell why.

99

What are three other numbers that might be in the first group and not in the second group? Why?

132	374		133	371
242	583		245	580

Examining Animal Tracks

What are you measuring when you find the amount of surface something covers?

How would you estimate the area of the skunk's hind foot track?

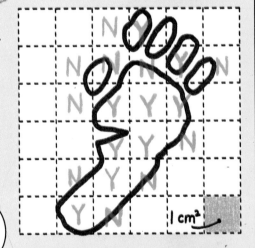

Clark traced it onto centimetre grid paper. Then he counted the squares where the track covered half or more.
He didn't count squares where the track covered less than half.

1. What is the approximate area in square centimetres (cm²) using this method?

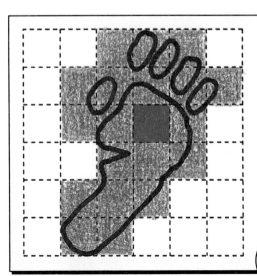

Arnie also traced it onto grid paper. He counted the squares that contained any part of the track. Then he counted the squares that were completely within the track. Then he found their average.

2. What is the approximate area using this method?

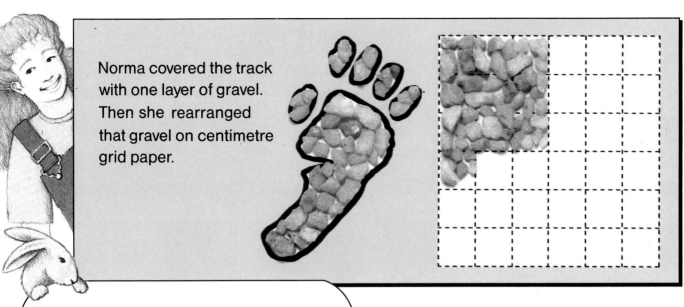

Norma covered the track with one layer of gravel. Then she rearranged that gravel on centimetre grid paper.

3. What is the approximate area using this method?

4. Which method do you prefer? Why? Can you think of any other methods?

Work in a group.

Use centimetre grid paper.

5. Estimate the area of each track using two methods. Which track do you think belongs to each animal?

cat   dog   cottontail rabbit   muskrat   beaver

What does $\frac{1}{4}$ size mean? Why is it used?

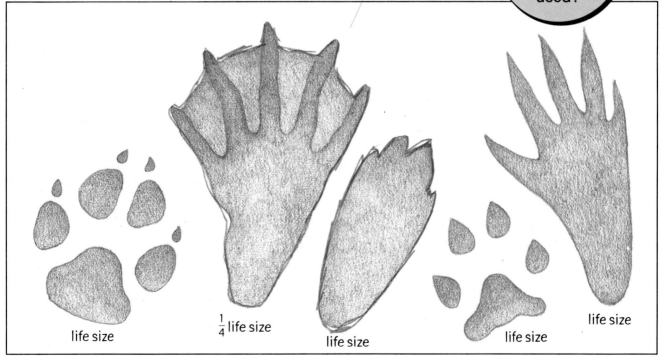

life size

$\frac{1}{4}$ life size

life size

life size

life size

6. What are some of the features that make the animal tracks different? Which of those differences are mathematical?

Irene is multiplying 36 and 15.
She thinks 36 × 10 = 360 and 5 is half of 10.
How might she use this to find 36 × 15?

Exploring Perimeter

Measuring perimeter of irregular shapes

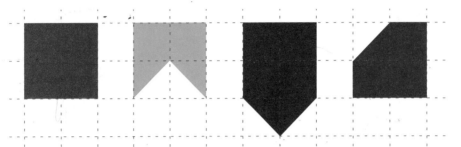

1. Find the square's perimeter in millimetres and its area in square centimetres.

2. Do you think the green figure's perimeter is greater or less than the square's? Measure to check. How do the areas compare?

3. Do you think the blue figure's perimeter is greater than or less than the square's? Measure to check. How do the areas compare?

4. What's the area of the purple figure? Estimate and then measure its perimeter.

Work with a partner.

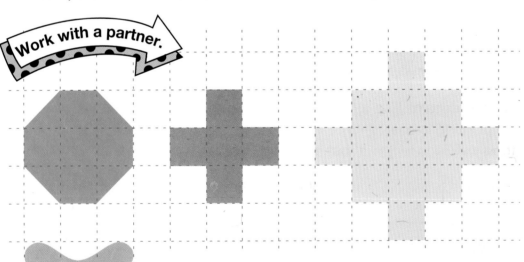

5. Find the perimeter of a 3 cm by 3 cm square. Estimate which of these four figures has a perimeter of 120 mm? greater than 120 mm? less than 120 mm? Find each perimeter.

6. Which perimeters in Problem 5 were easiest to find? Explain.

7. Cut 30 cm of string. Make a figure on grid paper. Trace its outline. Compare your figure's shape and area with several classmates'. What do you notice?

102

You can only travel on grid lines.
Find a point that is twice as far from (2,3) as from (5,4). Is there more than one?

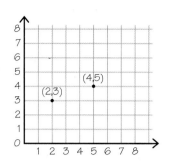

Measuring Wheels

Examining circumference and diameter

Use any wheel.
What distance is covered when it makes one complete turn?

1. Tell what you did find out.
   What else could you do to find out?

2. What is the perimeter of a circular object like a wheel called?

3. What is the distance across the circular face through the centre called?
   Measure that distance on your wheel.

Work with a partner.

4. A wheel has a diameter of 10 cm. Sketch what you
   think the wheel looks like. Now measure to check.

5. A wheel has a circumference of 10 cm. Sketch the wheel.
   Use a 10 cm piece of string to check.
   Was your circle too small? too large? about right?

6. Which was easier to sketch, the circle in Problem 4 or Problem 5? Explain.

7. What is the circumference of the largest circle that will fit on a page in this
   book? Explain what you did to find out.

8. What unit would you use to measure the circumference of a Ferris wheel?
   a toy car wheel? an in-line skate wheel?

9. When might you use kilometres to measure circumference?

10. Smaller wheels must turn more often to cover the same distance as larger wheels.
    Explain why.

Multiply 38 and 99 in your head.
Explain to a classmate how you did it.

Modelling Sports Surfaces

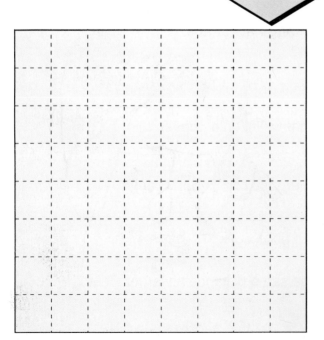

1 m²

Dimensions of Sports Surfaces	
Basketball	26 m × 14 m
Judo	16 m × 16 m
Karate	8 m × 8 m
Skating	60 m × 30 m
Swimming	50 m × 21 m
Wrestling	12 m × 12 m

Sonja made a model of one of the sports surfaces on grid paper.

Which sports surface did she model?

1. What is the area of the model in square centimetres (cm²)?
   What is the actual area in square metres (m²)?
   What is the perimeter of the model?
   What is the actual perimeter?

1 cm represents 1 m

1 cm² represents 1 m²

Use centimetre grid paper.

2. Model the other sports surfaces. Write the length and width of each.

3. Order the surfaces from greatest to least area. Tell how you decided the order.

4. Order the surfaces from greatest to least perimeter. Tell how you decided the order.

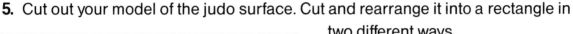

5. Cut out your model of the judo surface. Cut and rearrange it into a rectangle in two different ways.
   Do your rectangles and the square have the same area? the same perimeter? Explain.
   Why do you think the judo surface is square?

6. Cut a string the length of the perimeter for each of two other surfaces. Rearrange each string to make the area of

   • one greater than its original
   • the other less than its original

   Compare these shapes with the original surface.

7. If you know a surface has a perimeter of 60 m, would you know what shape it must be? Explain.

8. Construct a rectangle with a perimeter of 30 cm and an area of 26 cm². What are the dimensions of the rectangle? Keep the perimeter the same. What happens to the area if the length is increased? decreased?

9. Do a square and a rectangle with the same perimeter have the same area? Explain.

Take Your Pick

CUTTING CORNERS

Cut 2 cm² from one corner of a 4 cm by 4 cm square.

Cut 3 cm² from the next corner.
Cut 2 cm² from the next corner.
What is the greatest perimeter possible for the remaining shape?
What is the least perimeter?

FENCE ME IN

What is the shape of a rectangular pen that encloses an area of 25 m² using the least amount of fencing? Explain.

PAIRS OF RECTANGLES

By how much do the areas of these rectangles differ?
By how do the perimeters differ?

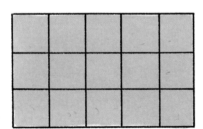
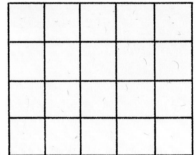

Draw another rectangle so that it and the green rectangle have areas differing by 10 cm² and perimeters differing by 4 cm.

Then draw another rectangle so that it and the yellow rectangle have areas differing by 4 cm² and perimeters differing by 2 cm.

GIVE ME A HAND

Estimate the area and perimeter of your hand. Then estimate the amount of fabric and thread to make a mitten for it.

30 PLEASE

Use a loop of string. On grid paper make as many different shapes as you can with a perimeter or circumference of 30 cm. Which appears to have the greatest area? the least?

Make up the other problems. Post them on the bulletin board for your classmates to solve.

List the first ten multiples of 8.
Add the digits of each multiple until a single digit results.
Describe the pattern.
Repeat this with the first ten multiples of 7.

Measuring the Volume of Food Boxes

Using cubic centimetres

Why do you think we say the volume of a unit cube is 1 cm³ (cubic centimetre)?

What are you measuring when you find volume?

What is the volume of a

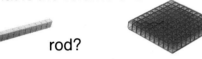

rod?   a flat?   a large cube?

1. What is the volume of this box?

Work with a partner.

Use base ten blocks to model food boxes.

2. Estimate and then find the volume of some of your food boxes.
List them from least to greatest volume.

3. Are most of the volumes less than or more than 100 cm³?

4. Estimate the volume of a large cereal box.
Which blocks would you use to help you find the volume?

5. Do you think that the volume of any box is the same as the volume of its contents?
Tell how you would find out.

About $\frac{1}{3}$ of our body mass is in our legs.

Estimate the mass of one of your legs in kilograms.

Building Boxes

Relating the volume of a box to its net

Here is the net of a box that is open on top.

How many cubes do you think will fit in the box?

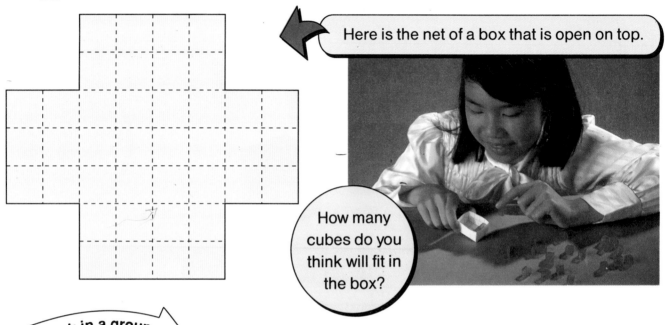

Work in a group.

Use centimetre grid paper and centimetre cubes.

1. Build an open box from each of these nets and the net above. Fill each with cubes.

What is the volume of each box in cubic centimetres?
How do the volumes compare? Explain.

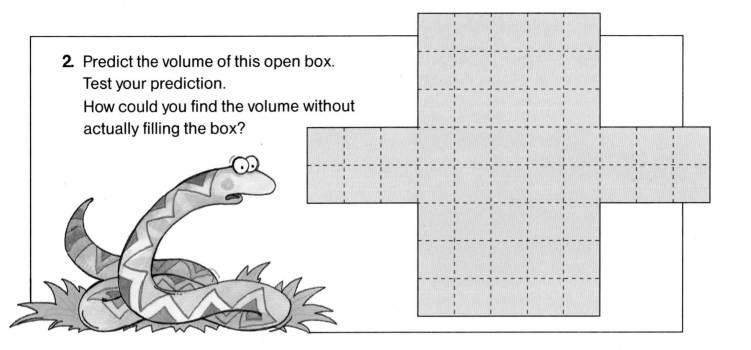

2. Predict the volume of this open box. Test your prediction.
How could you find the volume without actually filling the box?

3. How can you use the net to predict this box's height? length? width?

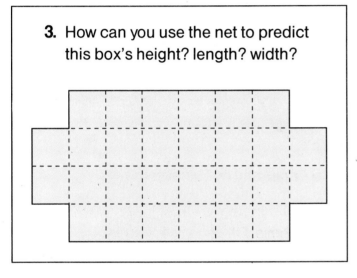

4. Build nets for open boxes with volumes of 13 cm³ and 17 cm³.
How many nets are possible for each box?
How are the nets alike?

5. Can you make a net for an open box with a volume of 21 cm³ that is 4 cm high? Explain.

6. Make a net for an open box that is twice as long, twice as wide, and twice as high as this one.
How do the volumes of the two boxes compare?

7. Brent said that counting the squares in the net tells you the volume of its box. Do you agree? Explain.

How could you use multiplication to find how many pennies would fit on the cover of your math book?

Filling Containers

Kelly is making a net for an open box using grid paper and cardboard. The box is to be 5 cm wide, 10 cm long, and 5 cm tall.

1. How many centimetre cubes will fit in the box? How do you know? What is the box's volume?

To measure capacity, Kelly filled the box with gravel. She then poured the gravel into a measuring cup.

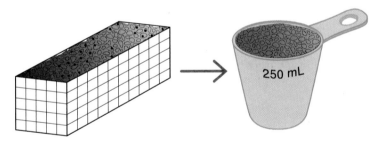

250 mL

The box holds 250 mL of gravel.

2. Relate the box's volume with its capacity. What do you notice?

Work in a group.

3. Look at the net at the top of page 108. What is the box's height? length? width? volume? Predict the capacity.
Copy the net and then build the box. Fill it with sand using a measuring spoon. How many millilitres does it hold?

4. Look at the other nets on pages 108 and 109. What is the volume of each box? Predict the capacity of each.
Build one and test your prediction by measuring its capacity.

5. You can often use volume to predict capacity. Explain.
Why might it be difficult to predict the capacity of a cooler from its volume?

110

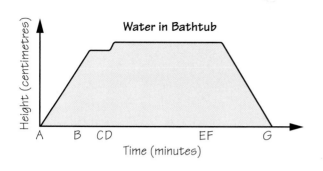

Water in Bathtub

Height (centimetres)

A   B   CD   EF   G

Time (minutes)

What might be happening at times A, B, C, D, E, F, and G?

Playing Measurement Match

Evaluating measurement units and tools

Emily created a measurement card game. She made sets of matching cards.

Each set of cards had

- a unit card

  millimetres (mm)

- a tool card

  ruler with millimetre units

- a situation card

  width of a button

1. Name four other units used to measure length. Why do you think the millimetre is the best unit to measure the button?

2. Name one tool and one situation for each of the four units from Problem 1. Compare your tools and situations with a classmate's.

Work in a group.

3. Create your own card game. Complete a set of three cards for each unit.

   - millilitre
   - litre

   - gram
   - kilogram

   - second
   - minute
   - hour
   - day
   - week
   - month
   - year
   - decade
   - century

   - square centimetre
   - square metre

   - Celsius degree

4. Make up rules for your game. You could play like the game of Fish or Rummy or make up your own game.

5. Which units are used to measure circumference or perimeter? volume? capacity? mass? area?

Tell five things about this shape.

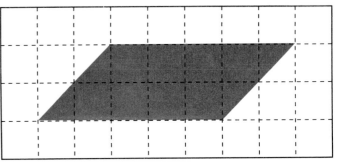

Comparing Dinosaur Masses

Would the kilogram be a good unit to measure the mass of a real dinosaur? Explain.

Would the gram be a better unit? Explain.

If you created a unit to measure the mass of a dinosaur, what would you call it? Why?

Sometimes, we use the **tonne** as a unit of mass.

How many kilograms is 1 t (tonne)?

Work with a partner.

Use the chart.

1. Express the mass of each dinosaur in kilograms.

Dinosaur	Mass
Brachiosaurus	77 t
Diplodocus	10.6 t
Stegosaurus	1.8 t
Triceratops	5.4 t
Tyrannosaurus	6.4 t

2. Which dinosaur is the heaviest? the lightest?

3. Would all the students in your class have as great a mass as any of the dinosaurs?
   What about all the students in your school? Which dinosaurs?

4. Trucks with a total mass of more than 36 000 kg are not allowed on some highways. Which of the dinosaurs wouldn't be allowed on these highways?

5. What else do you think might be measured in tonnes?

112

Take your pick

ELEVATORS

About how many tonnes can this elevator safely hold? Which is the best unit for this situation, tonne, gram, or kilogram? Explain.

MAXIMUM
16 occupants

CUPBOARD SPACE

Estimate the volume of the smallest cupboard in your classroom.

BASE TEN STRUCTURES

Use base ten blocks to build several different structures with a volume of 200 cm³. How high a structure can you build?

MAKING BOXES

Use centimetre grid paper. Cut out a 10 cm by 6 cm rectangle. Then cut one square out of each corner and fold to make an open box.

How many centimetre cubes will it hold? What is its capacity? Then cut three more squares out of each corner and fold to make an open box.

How many centimetre cubes will that box hold? Which open box has the greater capacity?

TWICE AS BIG

This solid is made with centimetre cubes. What is its volume?

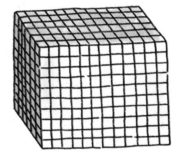

Another rectangular prism has a volume that is twice this. How long might its sides be?

Make up the other problems. Post them on the bulletin board for your classmates to solve.

Solving a Problem by Acting It Out

Try this problem before going on.

WATER LILY

The queen-size royal water lily in Brazil has leaves that are over 2 m across. About how many students can stand on a surface this size?

Art's group solved the problem by acting it out.

We made a cross with four metre sticks and a circle with string.

Then we removed the metre sticks and crowded our classmates into the circle.

Finish their work.

Work in a group.

Solve these problems by acting them out.

SHARING MASSES

One student is holding four 10 kg masses. Another student is holding four 5 kg masses. A third student is holding five 2 kg masses. A fourth student is holding six 1 kg masses. Can they share the masses so that each holds the same amount? If so, how?

ADDING ON

One student adds 1 cube to this solid. Each of 9 other students  adds 2 more cubes to it than the student before. What will the volume of the solid be when all of the students have added their cubes?

HANDSHAKES

Six friends meet. Each shakes hands with each of the others. How many handshakes are there?

114

1. Name something you might measure in each unit. What tool would you use for each?

   tonne   square centimetre   millimetre

   millilitre   cubic centimetre   square metre

2. Estimate the area of the first shape one way. Then estimate the area of the second shape a different way.

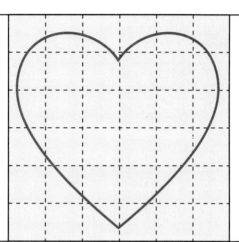 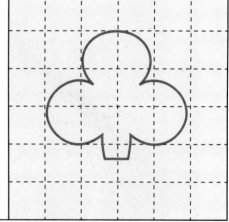

3. Make another rectangle with the same area but a greater perimeter.

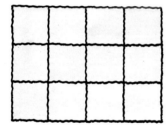

4. Use string to make a circle with the same perimeter as the rectangle shown in Problem 3. Describe the perimeter another way.

5. Copy the rectangle shown in Problem 3 onto grid paper. Draw a shape inside with a greater perimeter. How much greater is it?

6. What is the volume of this solid made from centimetre cubes?

   Make another shape with the same volume. Draw or describe it.

7. Which is more? Tell why.
   • 40 m² or 4000 cm²   • 2 t or 2000 kg

8. Make a net for an open box that will hold 20 mL.

Playing Games for Practice

Play each game in a group of 2, 3, or 4.

How High?

- Shuffle the base cards. Place them face down in a pile.
- Roll 2 dice to create a 2-digit number. The digits can be in either order.
- Take that number of cubes.
- Turn over a base card.
- Imagine a structure built on that base with the cubes you have.
- Estimate how many cubes high the structure would be at its tallest point.
- Build the structure to check your estimate.
- Score 1 point for being within 1 cube of the height,
    2 points for being the exact height.
- Take turns.
- The winner is the first player to reach a score of 10.

Example

25 used   5 cubes high estimated   Score 2 points.

Last One In

- Roll a die to get an area from 1 square unit to 6 square units.
- Color a shape with that area on a 10 by 10 grid.
- Take turns coloring shapes. Each player uses a different color.
- The winner is the last player to be able to color a shape.

Example

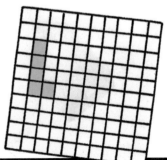

Take Your Pick

PACKING CARTONS

What is the capacity of this box? What size of box can be made to hold exactly 8 of these cartons? Identify the length, depth, and thickness of the carton.

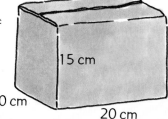

15 cm

10 cm

20 cm

CUTTING PAPER

Is the perimeter of half a sheet of paper $\frac{1}{2}$ of the perimeter of a whole sheet? Explain.
Would the perimeter of a third of a sheet of paper be $\frac{1}{3}$ of the perimeter of a whole sheet?

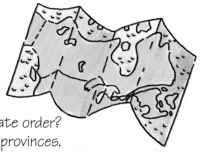

CANADA

Use a map of Canada.
For each province, trace the outline and cut it out.
Order the provinces from least to greatest area.
Why might tracing some provinces from one map and others from a different map not result in an accurate order?
Describe how you might compare the perimeters of the provinces.

CLASSROOM SPACE

About how many square centimetres does your desk take up? About how many square metres do all the student desks in your room take up?

CRACKERS

How many boxes are needed to have one tonne of crackers? Would that many boxes fit in your classroom? Explain.

FRISCUITS

250g

Make up the other problems. Post them on the bulletin board for your classmates to solve.

1. Which is the most reasonable measurement for the area of a window?

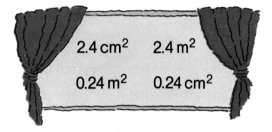

2.4 cm²   2.4 m²

0.24 m²   0.24 cm²

2. Rewrite the signs using kilograms and metres. Why are larger units useful?

LOAD LIMIT 16 t

KAMLOOPS 185 km

3. What unit would you most likely use to measure a bar of soap's volume? mass?

4. This garden is 8 m by 3 m. What is the garden's area? perimeter?

Could a different garden have
- the same perimeter, but more area? Explain.
- the same area, but more perimeter? Explain.

5. Describe a situation where you might measure circumference in
   - millimetres
   - centimetres
   - metres

   What tool would you use to measure each?

6. Find the area and perimeter of this kite. Tell how you did it.

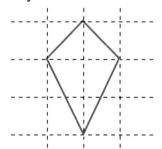

A rectangle has an area 20 times as great as this kite. Sketch a rectangle and show the side lengths possible. Is the perimeter 20 times as great? Explain.

7. A rectangular prism has a volume of 40 cm³ Make a model. Draw a net on grid paper of an open box with the same volume. What is its capacity?

Make a model of a rectangular prism with $\frac{1}{8}$ the capacity.

118

Thinking Back

Use two rectangles. Show why the rectangle with the greater area is not necessarily the one with the greater perimeter.

Explain to someone two different methods you might use to find the area of the sole of your foot. How would you find its perimeter?

What would you name a distance of 1000 km? Why? Is such a unit useful?

The volume of this cube is 24 mL.

Tell two things that are wrong with this statement.

How would you determine the number of math books needed to make a mass of one tonne?

What questions do you still have about measurement?

Examining

▼ What number is shown?

represents one

Use base ten blocks. Compared to this number, show a number that is
- 1000 less
- 2000 greater
- twice as great
- half as great

▼ What number is shown in the row of blocks? in the array of blocks?

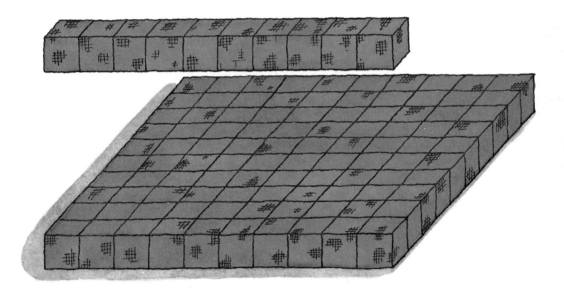

◀ Why do you think millimetre and millilitre both start with *milli*?
What do you think *milli* means?
What other words do you know that start with *milli*?

Large Numbers

▶ How many bills would this be if the prize was all in $1000 bills? $100 bills? $10 bills?

THIS IS TO CERTIFY THAT ZOE PLOUSOS WON $10 000

To claim your prize, read the instructions that follow.

▼ What is the greatest number you have ever seen written?
What did the number tell about?

PRINCE RUPERT 148 km

REAL ESTATE NEWS

40 000 FANS AT SKYDOME WATCH THE BLUE JAYS WORLD SERIES

SPORTS

ST. JOHN'S POP. 96 200

Two of the digits in a 3-digit number are 6 and 7. The number is a multiple of 3. What could it be?

Collecting Pop Can Tabs

Caroline's Guide company collects pop can tabs. They put 100 tabs in a small bag. Then they put 10 small bags in a large bag.

How many tabs are in a large bag?

What base ten block represents the number of tabs in a small bag? in a large bag?

This model shows how many tabs Caroline's company collected.

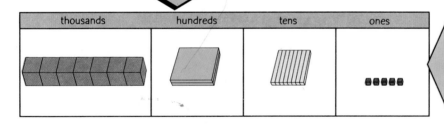

thousands	hundreds	tens	ones

1. How many tabs did they collect? How many large bags do they have? small bags not in large bags? leftover tabs?

Model using base ten blocks.

2. Another Guide company collected 3456 tabs. Model this. How many large bags do they have? small bags not in large bags? leftover tabs?

3. Another Guide company has 7 large bags, 3 small bags, and some leftover tabs. How many tabs altogether might this company have? Model that number.

4. How many large bags are needed for 10 000 tabs? How can you show 10 000 using base ten blocks? Do these three companies have 10 000 tabs?

Model using base ten blocks.

5. How many tabs has each
Scout troop collected?
Which troop has collected
the most tabs?
How can you tell?

1st Pickering Scout Troop

2nd Pickering Scout Troop

3rd Pickering Scout Troop

6. The 3rd Pickering Troop gets two more
tabs. What can they do now?

7. About how many tabs have all three
troops collected?

8. Ten large bags
are put in a box.
How many tabs
are in a box?
How would you model that number?

9. A row of 10 large cubes is sometimes
called a big long. A 10 by 10 array
of large cubes is sometimes called a
big flat. How many tabs would a
big flat represent?

10. This model shows the
number of tabs one
Guide district collected.
How many tabs does this
represent?
Write a number that shows
• 10 000 less tabs   • 100 000 less tabs

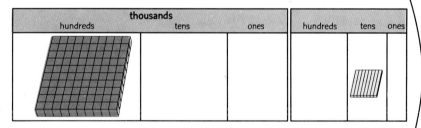

thousands					
hundreds	tens	ones	hundreds	tens	ones

11. One Guide company collected this many tabs. How many is this?

The number of tabs collected by a Scout troop has the same 5 digits
but in a different order.
Could they have collected more than 30 000?   less than 10 000?

12. Do you know any Guide, Scout, or other groups that collect pop can
tabs? Why do they collect them?

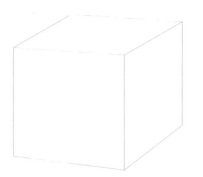

What is the fewest number of colors needed to color a cube so that faces that share edges have different colors?

Comparing Canadian Communities

City*/Town, Province	Population (1991)
Grand Falls-Windsor, Nfld	14 693
Charlottetown*, PEI	15 396
Sydney*, NS	26 063
Bathurst*, NB	14 409
Baie-Comeau*, Que.	26 012
Milton, Ont.	32 075
Brandon*, Man.	38 567
Estevan*, Sask.	10 240
Fort Saskatchewan*, Alta	12 078
Terrace, B.C.	11 433

CHARLOTTETOWN
Population 15 396

BRANDON
Population 38 567

TERRACE
Population 11 433

1. Which population is modelled here?

thousands					
hundred	ten	one	hundreds	tens	ones
	1	2		7	8

You would read and write this number as "twelve thousand, seventy-eight".
You could also write the numeral, 12 078.

2. Suppose 100 people moved into this community. What's the new population? Write the number word and numeral.

3. Record the numeral for Bathurst's population on a place value chart. How does it compare to Fort Saskatchewan's population? Explain how you compared.

4. Record the numeral for Grand Falls-Windsor's population on a place value chart. How does it compare to Bathurst's population? Explain how you compared.

Work with a partner.

5. Record each population on a place value chart. Then write each number word.

   Sydney   Baie-Comeau   Milton   Brandon

6. Which population in each pair is greater?

   • Brandon and Baie-Comeau   • Brandon and Milton   • Sydney and Baie-Comeau

7. Which pair in Problem 6 was most difficult to compare? Explain.

8. Order the populations in Problem 5 from least to greatest.

9. Order the communities in the chart from greatest to least population.

10. Do cities have greater populations than towns? Explain.

11. Medicine Hat, Alberta had forty-three thousand, six hundred twenty-five people in 1991. Write the numeral.

12. Arrange the digits in Medicine Hat's population to make the
    • greatest number possible
    • least number possible
    • a population greater than Sydney's but less than Brandon's
    • a population less than Brandon's but greater than Milton's

13. Write the numeral for Medicine Hat's population if
    • 6 moved in   • 30 moved out   • 500 moved in
    • 4000 moved out   • 20 000 moved in   • the population doubled

14. Write the number word and numeral for
    • the greatest 5-digit whole number
    • the least 6-digit whole number

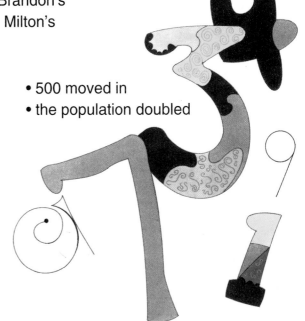

How many blue bags would balance one yellow bag?

Examining Our Diet

On average in half a day, Canadians eat

98 882 kg of processed cheese

42 449 kg of cottage cheese

71 148 kg of fresh broccoli

40 425 kg of peanut butter

Peter is estimating the number of kilograms of cottage and processed cheese eaten on an average half day.

cottage cheese
42 449 is a bit over 40 thousand
processed cheese
98 882 is almost 99 thousand

Finish his estimate. Is it high or low? Explain.

What other numbers could you have used to estimate? Can you add them in your head?

Kate is estimating how many more kilograms of cottage cheese than peanut butter are eaten on an average half day.

cottage cheese
42 449 is a bit over 42 thousand
peanut butter
40 425 is a bit over 40 thousand

Finish her estimate. Is it high or low? Explain.

What other numbers could you have used to estimate?

Can you subtract them in your head?

126

Use the data about what Canadians eat.

1. On an average half day, about how many more kilograms are eaten of
   - processed cheese than cottage cheese?
   - broccoli than peanut butter?

2. On an average half day, about how many kilograms of cottage cheese and peanut butter are eaten?

3. How would you estimate the number of kilograms of cottage cheese eaten per hour? Estimate the number of kilograms of cottage cheese eaten per hour. Is your estimate high or low? Explain.

4. Peter is estimating how many more kilograms of processed cheese than broccoli are eaten in half a day.

   98 882 kg of processed cheese is about 98 000. 71 148 kg of broccoli is about 71 000 kg.

   Why did he use these numbers? Finish his estimate. Is it high or low? Explain.

5. About what fraction of half a day does it take Canadians to eat 50 000 kg of broccoli?

   50 000 = 50 thousand

   broccoli
   71 148 is almost 75 thousand

6. About how many tonnes of peanut butter are eaten on an average half day? processed cheese? broccoli? cottage cheese?

7. Every minute, Canadians drink about 5400 L of milk. About how many glasses is that?

8. Make up 3 problems about the data for another group to solve.

9. How do you think this data might have been gathered?

What addition might have been done?
What subtraction might have been done?

Going to School Around the World

Country	Number of Elementary Schools
Australia	8 442
Canada	9 307
England	24 609
Japan	24 901
Mexico	80 518
United States	71 608

Fran is calculating how many less schools there are in Canada than in Mexico.

First she estimates.

80 518 is about 81 thousand
9307 is about 9 thousand
81 thousand — 9 thousand = 72 thousand

Then she calculates.

C 8 0 5 1 8 − 9 3 0 7 =

Why did she estimate before using the calculator?

Work with a partner.

Estimate and then calculate.

1. How many more schools are there in England than in Canada?

2. In Canada and the United States, what is the total number of schools? How does this compare to the number of schools in Mexico?

3. About how many times as many schools are there in England as there are in Australia?

4. How many fewer schools are there in England than Japan?

5. Make up two problems about the data for another group to solve.

IMMAGRATION

Number of Immigrants to Canada in a Typical Day

European	142
African	37
Australasian	7
Asian	304
North and Central American	70
South American	24

About how many immigrants come to Canada in 5 months?
About half of the immigrants settle in Ontario.
About how many is that?

SLINKYS

62 500 Slinkys
are sold in Canada in
3 months.
About how many are
sold each day?

MULTIPLICATION

If you multiply a 3-digit number by a 2-digit number,
how many digits are likely in the product? Explain.

MONEY, MONEY, MONEY

Bankruptcies in Canada, 1988–1993

1988	33 848
1989	37 866
1990	54 424
1991	75 773
1992	76 139
1993	66 983

Have bankruptcies increased every year
since 1988? Explain.

ONES AND NINES

Each digit in a 5-digit number is
either a 1 or a 9.
What is the number if it is as close
as possible to 10 000? 100 000?
Write both number words.

Make up other problems. Post them
on the bulletin board for your
classmates to solve.

Solving a Problem by Finding Needed Information

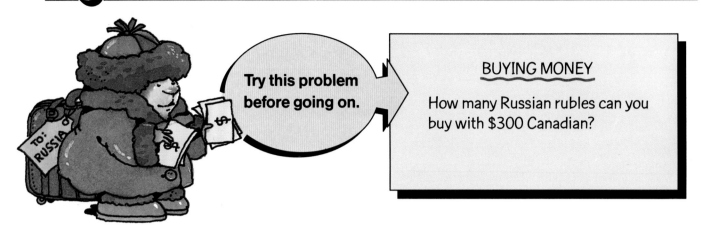

Try this problem before going on.

BUYING MONEY

How many Russian rubles can you buy with $300 Canadian?

Pat's group solved this problem by finding needed information.

○   ○

We called a bank to find out the exchange rate.
We learned that $1 Canadian buys 333 Russian rubles.

$1 buys 333 rubles
So $300 buys   333 × 300 rubles
            = 99 900 rubles

Work in a group.

Solve these problems by first finding the needed information.

RAISINS

About how many individual serving boxes do you need to get 100 000 raisins?

TO AND FROM

About how many times would you have to travel to and from school to cover the distance between New York City and London England?

COUNTING CANADIANS

Find the difference between the populations of 2 towns in your province with less than 100 000 people.

1. Write each number in words.   20 000   95 700   100 000

2. Write each number as a numeral.
   - two thousand
   - eighty-five thousand
   - ninety-three thousand, nine hundred ninety-eight

3. How many thousands of dollars is each week's sales?

   February Sales

Week 1	$20 000
Week 2	$52 000
Week 3	$76 000
Week 4	$91 000

4. What is 100 000 in
   - thousands?
   - tens?

5. Order these numbers from least to greatest.

14 013	43 125	0.25
32 513	40 012	0.30

6. Can you walk 100 000 mm? Explain.

7. Find the next three numbers in the pattern.

   13 567   14 567   15 567

8. The population in Town A is 23 300. The population in Town B is 51 900. Estimate the difference in population, then calculate.

Playing Games

Play each game in a group of 2, 3, or 4.

Deal Numbers

- Remove the face cards and aces from a deck of playing cards.
- Shuffle the cards and deal 5 to each player.
- Form the greatest 5-digit number possible using your cards.
- Then score, depending on your number,

  1 point if it is even

  2 points if it is a multiple of 5

  3 points if it is greater than 70 000

  5 points if it rounds to 50 000
- Play until one player has 25 points.

Example

55 432   even   1 point
Score 1 point

Variations:
- Make the least number possible.
- Change the scoring.

Limit 10 000

- Remove the face cards and aces from a deck of playing cards.
- Shuffle the cards and deal one card face up to each player.
- Then deal one card at a time, face up, to each player until the player says to stop.
- Say stop when you estimate that the product of your numbers is close to, but not greater than, 10 000.
- When all players have said stop, use a calculator to check each multiplication.
- The player closest to 10 000 but not greater than scores 5 points.
- Continue until one player has 25 points.

Example

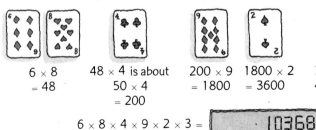   STOP

6×8 48×4 is about 200×9 1800×2 3600×3 is about
$= 48$ 50×4 $= 1800$ $= 3600$ 4000×3
        $= 200$ $= 12 000$

$6 \times 8 \times 4 \times 9 \times 2 \times 3 =$ 10368

Variation: Use a different number, such as 50 000.

Take Your Pick

SUM AND DIFFERENCE

Use any digits except 0 to form two numbers with a sum close to 90 000 and a difference close to 20 000. Find another pair of numbers.

HOW OLD?

Are you older than 100 000 minutes? Explain.

CANADIAN FAMILIES

Number of Children	Number of Families (to the nearest thousand)
5	41 000
6	12 000
7	4 000
8	3 000

About how many families have
- 5 or more children?
- 5 or 6 children?
- 8 or more children?

About how many times as many children have five brothers or sisters as children who have six brothers or sisters?

EVENS AND ODDS

The red square must be an even digit. The blue squares must be odd digits. What number is as close as possible to 50 000?

CALCULATOR SURPRISE

What digits occur in the answers?

75 × 231   65 × 281
86 × 251   87 × 435

Make up other problems. Post them on the bulletin board for your classmates to solve.

1. Write a numeral for
   • a number between 50 thousand and 100 thousand
   • a number a little greater than 43 thousand

2. Use the digits from 1 to 5 to create a number less than 60 000 but greater than 53 000. Write the number word.

3. A number less than 30 000 is subtracted from a number greater than 80 000. What do you know about the difference?

4. In Canada, there are 51 966 doctors, 1226 hospitals.

   How many times as many doctors are there as hospitals?

5. An ice cream sundae made in Edmonton in 1988 had a mass of 24 908 kg. It contained

   20 270.7 kg of ice cream,
   4394.4 kg of syrup,
   234.7 kg of topping.

   How much more syrup was there than topping?

6. How many $20 bills are equal to $100 000?
   How do you know?

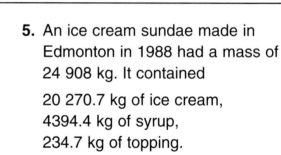

7. A square has an area of 10 000 cm². What is the length of each side in centimetres? metres?

Thinking Back

When might you need to subtract two 5-digit numbers to find an exact answer? When would an estimate do? Explain.

Create a pair of 4-digit numbers which would be easy to compare.

Create another pair which would be difficult to compare.

Write a list of instructions which would help someone compare your second pair of numbers.

Do you think there is a greatest number?
Why or why not?

When might 1000 of something be greater in some way than 100 000 of something else?

When have you seen a hundred thousand of something?
Tell about it.

What questions do you still have about large numbers?

Introducing Probability

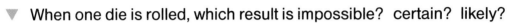

▼ When one die is rolled, which result is impossible? certain? likely?
- either an odd number or an even number
- a number greater than 6
- a number less than 5

▼ Which is more likely to happen when a coin is tossed 100 times? Explain.

- always heads
- always tails
- heads about $\frac{1}{4}$ of the time
- tails about $\frac{1}{2}$ of the time

◀ A new boy joins your class. Which prediction about him is most likely to be true? Why?
- His birthday is March 21.
- He is 10 years old.
- He has 7 brothers and 5 sisters.
- His name is Fred.

HEADS	TAILS
‖‖‖	‖‖

8   10   6   8

◀ Explain how you could find the average number in each pile without calculating.

▼ Which statements are true about the average height of this family?
- less than 160 cm
- between 120 cm and 140 cm
- less than 120 cm

Use the phrase *"the average is about"* to describe
- the age of the students in your class
- the number of students in the classes at your school
- the length of pencils used by students in your class

160 cm   100 cm   120 cm   140 cm

How many cubes are needed to build this cube?
What numbers of cubes can be used to build larger cubes?
What do you notice about these numbers?

Playing Baseball

Eryn either strikes out or hits a home run each time she is at bat. One outcome is as likely as the other.

Predict how many home runs and strikeouts she will likely have after 10 times at bat.

Bram is doing an experiment to simulate Eryn's performance at bat.
He writes SO on one slip of paper and HR on another.
Then he put the slips in a bowl.
He draws one slip, records the result, and puts the slip back in the bowl.
He does this 10 times.

1. How does your prediction compare with Bram's results?

Work with a partner.

2. Simulate Eryn's performance like Bram did.
   Compare your results
   • to Bram's
   • to those of 3 other pairs of students
   Tell what you notice.

138

3. Josh either strikes out or hits a home run. He strikes out twice as often as he hits a home run. Which set of slips should you use to simulate his performance at bat?

Predict. Then do an experiment to simulate each situation and check your prediction. Then compare your results with other pairs of students.

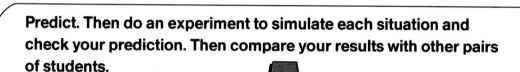

4. How many home runs and strikeouts will Josh likely have after 10 times at bat?

5. How many times at bat will Josh likely need to have 3 strikeouts in a row? What about Eryn?

6. Jesse either walks, strikes out, or hits a home run. How many home runs will she likely hit after 20 times at bat in each situation?

Example 1   Example 2   Example 3

For each situation, describe how likely each outcome is.

7. Use any of these outcomes and 5 slips of paper. You do not have to use all the outcomes.
   How often will a player likely walk after 20 times at bat?
   W (walk)   SO (strikeout)   HR (home run)

Find this sum.
696 + 986 + 686 + 818 + 969 + 919
Turn your book upside down and add the numbers you now see. What do you notice?

Predicting Weather in Chewandswallow
Using fractions to describe chance

In the land of Chewandswallow, it never rained rain. It never snowed snow. And it never blew just wind. It rained things like soup and juice. It snowed mashed potatoes and green peas. And sometimes the wind blew in storms of hamburgers.

from *Cloudy with a Chance of Meatballs* by Judi Barrett and Ron Barrett

You can simulate the weather by doing an experiment.

Work in a group.

Use grid paper to record your results for a 30-day month. Compare your answers with other groups.

1. Roll a die 30 times and use these outcomes to simulate the weather for April in Chewandswallow.
   - An even number is pancakes.
   - An odd number is syrup.

   How many days did it snow pancakes? rain syrup?

   What fraction of the days did it snow pancakes? rain syrup?

2. Which fraction best describes the probability of snowing pancakes in April? Why?

$\frac{1}{30}$ $\qquad$ $\frac{1}{10}$ $\qquad$ $\frac{1}{5}$ $\qquad$ $\frac{1}{2}$

3. If the weather was similar to April for the entire year, about how many days would it likely snow pancakes?

4. Roll a die 30 times and use these outcomes to simulate the weather for June in Chewandswallow.
   • A number greater than 1 is spaghetti.
   • A number greater than 2 is meat sauce.
   • The number 6 is grated cheese.

How many days did it rain spaghetti? meat sauce? grated cheese? all three foods? no food?

What fraction tells the probability of raining spaghetti? meat sauce? grated cheese? all three foods? no food?

5. Roll a die 30 times and use these outcomes to simulate the weather for September in Chewandswallow.
   • An even number is hamburger patties.
   • A multiple of 3 is buns.
   • The number 2 is ketchup.

What fraction tells the probability of raining hamburger patties? buns? ketchup? hamburger patties and buns? no food?

Why is raining hamburger patties more probable than raining ketchup?

Why is raining all three foods impossible or will never happen?

6. Choose a food that you like and one that you don't like. Make up a probability rule for one die so that more days in November will rain the food you like than the one you don't like. Simulate the weather to check.

Your femur or thigh bone makes up about one quarter of your height.
Estimate its length.

Examining Probability Experiments

Exploring effects of age and skill by displaying data in a variety of ways

Kyle's group conducted a coin tossing experiment. They predicted 25 heads in 50 tosses. They displayed their results in a variety of ways.

Tally and Frequency Table

	after this number of tosses					
	10	20	30	40	50	Total
Heads	⫴⫴ II	IIII	⫴⫴ I	⫴⫴	⫴⫴ II	29
Tails	II I	⫴⫴	III I	⫴⫴ III	I	21

Line Graph

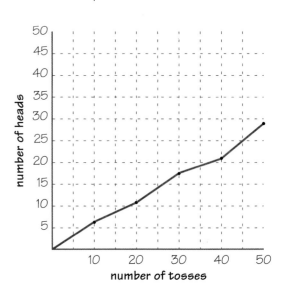

Frequency Bar Graph

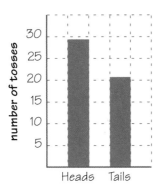

1. What information does the table and line graph give you that the bar graph doesn't?

2. What would a line graph for the number of tails tossed look like?

3. Why did Kyle's group predict 25 heads? How did the results compare with the prediction?

4. If Kyle's group continued to experiment with coins, would they improve their ability to toss exactly 25 heads in 50 tosses? Explain.

Work in a group.

5. What are the possible outcomes of tossing a tack?

6. Toss a tack 10 times to see how often it lands "point up".
Predict the number of "points up" in 50 tosses.

142

7. Conduct a tack tossing experiment. Display your results in three ways.

 • a tally and frequency table   • a line graph   • a bar graph

8. How did the results compare to your prediction? to results of other groups?

9. Suppose an adult tossed the tack. Would he or she be more able to toss the predicted number of "points up"? Explain.

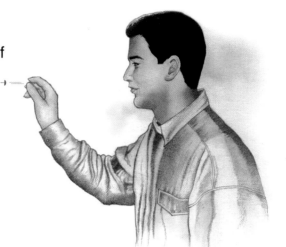

10. What are the possible outcomes of rolling a die? What fraction of the outcomes are prime numbers? composite numbers? not prime or composite?

11. Predict the number of times you will roll a prime number in 36 rolls. Explain your prediction.

12. Conduct a die rolling experiment. Display your results in a tally and frequency table, a line graph, and a bar graph.

13. How did your results compare to your prediction?

14. Is there anything you could have done to make sure you rolled the predicted number of prime numbers? Explain.

15. Some games are like probability experiments. A game of chance is one for which the outcome can't be predicted and age and skill have no effect.
Name several games of chance that you have played.

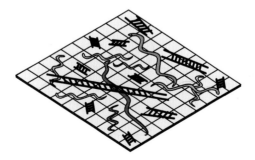

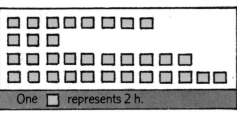

Hours of TV Watched in One Week

Gabe	☐☐☐☐☐☐☐☐
Doreen	☐☐☐
Jonah	☐☐☐☐☐☐☐☐☐
Rachel	☐☐☐☐☐☐☐☐☐☐☐

One ☐ represents 2 h.

Make up 5 questions about the pictograph for a classmate to answer.

How does your TV viewing compare with this data?

Choosing a Student

Calculating expected probabilities

One student is needed to take the hamsters home for the holidays.
Ten students volunteer.
The class decides to write each volunteer's name on a slip of paper.
The volunteer whose name is chosen gets to take care of the hamsters.

Why does each name have an equal chance of being chosen?

By calculating, the probability of choosing a name starting with A is $\frac{1}{2}$ because 5 out of 10 names start with A.

$$\frac{5}{10} = \frac{1}{2}$$

1. Calculate the probability of choosing Anna. Explain.

Work in a group.

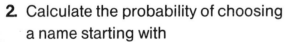

2. Calculate the probability of choosing a name starting with

B   D   J   R

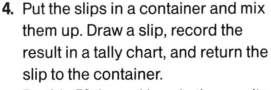

4. Put the slips in a container and mix them up. Draw a slip, record the result in a tally chart, and return the slip to the container.
Do this 50 times. How do the results of the experiment compare with the calculated probability?

3. Write the first name of each student in your group on a slip of paper.
Calculate the probability of choosing
  • your name
  • a name with more than 5 letters

5. List the first names of the students in your class. Calculate the probability of choosing a name that
  • begins with a letter from A to M
  • has at least 2 letters
  • begins with a vowel
  • has an even number of letters

144

Take Your Pick

BOARD GAMES

In some board games, you get an extra turn by rolling a double with a pair of dice.

Predict the probability of rolling a double.

Roll a pair of dice 30 times. Check your prediction.

PHONE NUMBER DIGITS

List the phone numbers of 10 students in your class.

Calculate the probability of choosing a phone number containing

- a 0
- 7 digits
- all different digits

CHOOSE A SPINNER

Which spinner was most likely used to get this result from 10 spins? Explain.
Is it possible to get this result using the other spinners?

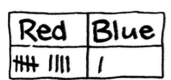

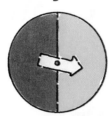 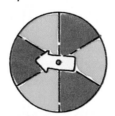 

SAMPLING CANDIES

About what fraction of the candies in the bin are likely yellow?

What is the probability of choosing a blue candy from the bin?

Could there be more than 4 colors in the bin? Explain.

Color of Candies Taken from Bin

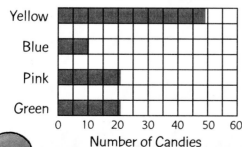

PLAYING HEADSY

In the game of Headsy, you get 2 points for tossing a Head and 1 point for a Tail. The first player to get more than 30 points wins.

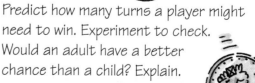

Predict how many turns a player might need to win. Experiment to check. Would an adult have a better chance than a child? Explain.

Make up other problems. Post them on the bulletin board for your classmates to solve.

Use your calculator. Complete this multiplication sentence using each of the other digits from 1 to 9 once.

[?]38 × [?][?] = [?][?][?]6

Examining Comic Strips

Graphing to find averages

Dolores made this graph.

Which statements are true? Explain.

The average number of letters in these titles is
- between 2 and 19
- close to 10
- close to 5
- close to 15

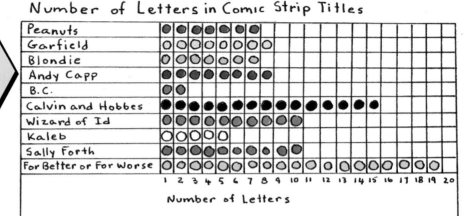

Number of Letters in Comic Strip Titles

	1	2	3	4	5	6	7	8	9	10	11	12	13	14	15	16	17	18	19	20
Peanuts	●	●	●	●	●	●	●													
Garfield	○	○	○	○	○	○	○													
Blondie	◐	◐	◐	◐	○	○														
Andy Capp	●	●	●	●	●	●	●	●												
B.C.	●	●																		
Calvin and Hobbes	●	●	●	●	●	●	●	●	●	●	●	●	●	●	●	●				
Wizard of Id	◐	◐	◐	◐	◐	◐	◐	◐	◐	◐										
Kaleb	○	○	○	○	○															
Sally Forth	●	●	●	●	●	●	●	●	●	●	●									
For Better or For Worse	○	○	○	○	◐	○	○	○	○	○	○	○	◐	○	○	○	○	○		

Number of Letters

Number of Letters in Comic Strip Titles

	1	2	3	4	5	6	7	8	9	10	11	12	13	14	15	16	17	18	19	20
Peanuts	◐	◐	◐	◐	◐	◐	◐	◐	○											
Garfield	○	○	○	○	○	○	○	○	○											
Blondie	○	○	○	○	○	○	○	○	○											
Andy Capp	●	●	●	●	●	●	●	●	●	○										
B.C.	●	○	●	○	●	●	●	●	●											
Calvin and Hobbes	●	●	●	●	●	●	●	●	●											
Wizard of Id	◐	●	◐	○	◐	◐	◐	◐	○											
Kaleb	○	○	○	○	○	●	●	○	○											
Sally Forth	●	●	●	●	●	●	●	●	○											
For Better or For Worse	○	○	○	○	○	○	○	○	○	○										

Number of Letters

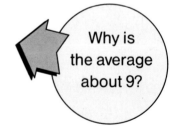

Dolores rearranged the counters to make each comic strip show about the same number of letters.

Why is the average about 9?

Work in a group.

Use at least 6 comic strips from a newspaper.
Answer 4 of the following questions.

What is the average number, to the nearest whole number, of

1. different characters?
2. sections?
3. speech balloons?
4. words?
5. punctuation marks?
6. pictures of animals?

Solving a Problem by Drawing a Diagram

Try this problem before going on.

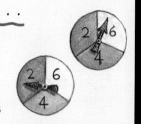

THE PROBABILITY IS . . .

For this pair of spinners, calculate the probability of getting
• a sum of 6
• the same number on both spinners

Shauna's group solved the problem by drawing a tree diagram.

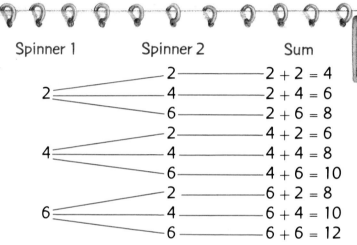

Spinner 1	Spinner 2	Sum
2	2	2 + 2 = 4
	4	2 + 4 = 6
	6	2 + 6 = 8
4	2	4 + 2 = 6
	4	4 + 4 = 8
	6	4 + 6 = 10
6	2	6 + 2 = 8
	4	6 + 4 = 10
	6	6 + 6 = 12

First we need to find all the possible outcomes.

2 out of the 9 possible outcomes give a sum of 6.

The probability of getting a sum of 6 is $\frac{2}{9}$.

3 out of the 9 possible outcomes show the same number on both spinners.

Finish their work.

Then calculate the probability of getting a sum of

10   12   14

Work in a group.

Solve these problems by drawing a tree diagram.

SPEAKING NUMBERS

Two students each say a number from 1 to 4. Calculate the probability that they will both say the same number.

SWITCH POSITIONS

How many different ways can the 3 light switches be positioned?

Calculate the probability that they will all be ON.

TOSSING DICE

How many sums can be tossed with a pair of dice? Calculate the probability of getting a sum of
2   6   7   10
Why do you think 7 is considered a lucky number?

1. Predict how many times the printing on a hexagonal pencil will be on the bottom when the pencil is rolled 24 times. Experiment to check. Did your age and skill affect the results? Explain.

2. Design a colored spinner where the probability of spinning blue is
$$\frac{1}{2} \qquad \frac{1}{4} \qquad 1 \qquad 0$$

3. Each coin of play money was tossed 1000 times.
   Which coin is probably not a fair one?

H	T
8	992

H	T
495	505

4. Calculate the probability of spinning an even number.

5. Show how to use the graph to find the average length of the ski trails.

   Cross Country Ski Trails

Meadow View	
Pine Valley	
Evergreen Alley	
Deer	
Hill Top	
Jack Rabbit	

   Each ▱ represents 1 km.

6. A card is picked from a deck of playing cards. Which prediction about the card has the greatest chance of being correct? Explain.

   It's a diamond.   It's a Jack.   It's the Jack of diamonds.

7. Predict how many times a factor of 12 will be rolled in 36 rolls. Experiment to check. Display your results in a table and graph.

8. The average price of 4 marking pens is $1. But not one pen costs exactly $1. Does this seem reasonable? Explain.

9. What sums are possible using this pair of spinners?

   Would you say *impossible, certain,* or *likely* to describe the probability that the sum is
   an even number?   an odd number?
   less than 16?   equal to 7, 9, or 11?

Playing Games for Practice

Play each game in a group of 3 or 4.

Making Choices

- Player 1 rolls a die 3 times and finds the sum.
- The other players take turns predicting whether they will roll a sum greater than, less than, or equal to the first sum rolled.
- After predicting, the players roll and test their predictions.
- Score 1 point to each player making a correct prediction
  - 1 point to Player 1 for each other player's incorrect prediction
- Take turns being Player 1. The first player to reach 10 points wins.

Example

Player 1	Player 2 Prediction: greater than 13	Player 3 Prediction: less than 13
  Sum = 13 Score 2 points (because Players 2 and 3 both made incorrect predictions).	 Sum = 10 Score 0 points.	 Sum = 14 Score 0 points.

On a Roll

- Roll a pair of dice and add the digits.
- Score 4 points for 2 or 12
  - 3 points for 3, 4, 5, 9, 10, or 11
  - 2 points for 6, 7, or 8
  - 1 extra point for doubles
- Take turns. The first player to reach 30 points wins.

Example

4 + 1 = 5

1 + 2 = 3

5 + 6 = 11

all 3 sums are worth 3 points each

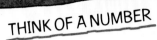

THINK OF A NUMBER

Each of 20 students thinks of a number from 0 to 9. The students work in pairs. Predict how many times the sum of the partners' numbers will be less than or equal to 10. Do an experiment to check your prediction.

NAMING COINS

Eric has 3 coins. The average value of the coins is 10¢. What coins does he have?

AVERAGE DISTANCE

The average distance from school to home for Hassan, Trina, and Jean is 6 km. Hassan lives 5 km from school and Trina lives 7 km from school. How far does Jean live from school?

HEADS AND TAILS

Three students predicted the results of tossing two pennies. Whose prediction will likely be correct the most number of times? Explain.

1 head and 1 tail

2 heads

2 tails

CREATING NUMBERS

Two spinners are spun to get two numbers.
The numbers are multiplied.
What products are possible?
Calculate the probability of the product being 0.

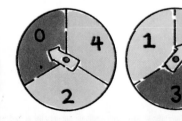

Make up other problems. Post them on the bulletin board for your classmates to solve.

Showing What You Know

1. In which city would a picnic for tomorrow be less likely to occur? Explain.

St. John's - cloudy tomorrow with a 10% chance of rain
Trois Rivières - cloudy tomorrow with a 90% chance of rain

2. Which statements mean the same?
   - It is certain.
   - It is impossible.
   - The probability is 0.
   - The probability is 1.

   Give an example of an outcome with a probability.
   - of 0
   - of 1

3. The average height of students in a class is 140 cm. When a new student joined the class, the average height stayed the same. How tall was the new student?

4. The chance of winning a prize is $\frac{1}{10}$. What does this mean?

5. Write each number from 1 to 10 on a slip of paper and place them in a bag. Predict the number of composite numbers drawn in 50 draws. Experiment to check. Display your results in a table and a graph.

6. You are shown the doors to 12 rooms and told
   - in 11 rooms there is a pot of gold you can keep
   - in 1 room there is a hungry tiger

   What is the chance of finding gold? Which of the two chances is the more improbable? Would you take the chance? Explain.

7. Calculate the probability of spinning
   - a B
   - an A
   Is there anything you could do to make sure a B is spun? Explain.

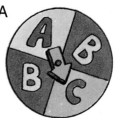

8. One marble is pulled out of a bag of 100 marbles. Its color is recorded and it is returned to the bag. This is done 10 times and the results are

   How many of each color of marble are probably in the bag?

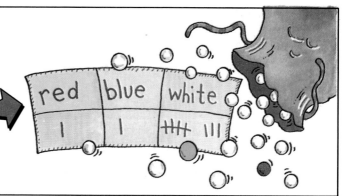

red	blue	white
I	I	⊮⊮ III

Compare the chances in the two draws.
What does this information tell you about buying lottery tickets?

Chances of winning first prize	1 in 14 000
Chances of winning first prize	1 in 4000

Make up a game of chance where age, experience, and skill have no effect on the results.

MATH TEST
JANUARY

MATH TEST
FEBRUARY

The average score on a January math test is 10. The average score on a February math test is 20. Is there enough information to tell if the students are doing better? Explain.

I get 1 point if the spinner stops on red. You get 2 points if it stops on blue.

Is this a fair game? Explain.

When might you display results in a table? a bar graph? a line graph?

What questions do you still have about probability?

UNIT
9

Investigating Structures

About how tall is an average 10-year-old?
About how tall is each building?
Compare the height of your school to the
heights of these buildings.
What shapes do you see here?
in your community?

153

HOW Can Numbers Describe Tall Structures?

Empire State Building

The Empire State Building in New York City is the world's best-known skyscraper. It opened in 1931, and was for many years the world's tallest building.

Facts
381 m high
102 storeys
1860 steps
73 elevators
15 000 workers
6500 windows
600 km of power cable
elevator speed 350 metres per minute
about 5500 visitors per day

1. About how high is each storey of the Empire State building?
   About how many steps are there between storeys?

2. On average, about how many visitors are there each week?

3. On average, about how many workers use each elevator?
   Do you think the number of elevators is reasonable? Explain.

Work with a partner.

4. The Petro-Canada Tower #2 in Calgary has 52 storeys and is 210 m high. Use this information to estimate the heights of these buildings.

Number of Storeys	
Royal Centre Tower, Vancouver	36
First Canadian Place, Toronto	72
Place Victoria, Montréal	47

Count the number of storeys in a building in your community.
Estimate the height of the building.

The CN Tower

The CN Tower in Toronto is the world's tallest free-standing structure, with a total height of 553 m. It was completed in 1976. The tower transmits communication signals, and is also a popular tourist centre. Each year, thousands of visitors ride in glassed-in elevators to a revolving restaurant and wide observation decks, which are 342 m above the ground.

5. The speed of the express elevators in the CN Tower is about 370 m/min. Do you think this is faster or slower than your walking speed? a car's speed on a city street?
   About how long would it take to go from the ground to the observation deck if the elevator didn't stop in between?
   About how long would it take you to walk the full 553 m height of the building if it were flat on the ground?

6. On a clear day, a visitor in the CN Tower can see about 100 km away. What cities or towns could you see if you could see 100 km from your school?

7. Choose the tallest structure in your community.
   Compare it to the Empire State Building or CN Tower in as many ways as you can.

Did you Know...?

Brendan Keenoy climbed the 1760 steps of the CN Tower in 1989 in 7 min 52 s.

▶ About how many times as fast as this is the elevator in the CN Tower?

How Much Mass Can a Bridge Support?

Work in a group.

1. Make a bridge connecting two stacks of books using an index card.
   Place a mass on the bridge. Measure the sag.

Remove the mass and place a second card on top of the first. Put the mass back on the bridge. Now measure the sag.

Try the same thing using three, four, and five cards. What do you notice?

> Create a graph showing the amount of sag for different numbers of cards.

2. Use four cards to build as strong a bridge as possible connecting the two stacks of books. Follow these rules:
   - The bridge must be at least 6 cm wide.
   - You may bend, fold, or cut the cards.
   - You may tape the cards to each other, but not to the books.
   - The bridge cannot touch the table. It can only touch the books.

   What is the maximum mass it can support?

3. Compare the bridges made.
   Which group has the best design?
   What makes it the best?

156

4. Make paper tubes of various lengths, distances across, and thicknesses. Test each as a bridge between two tables.

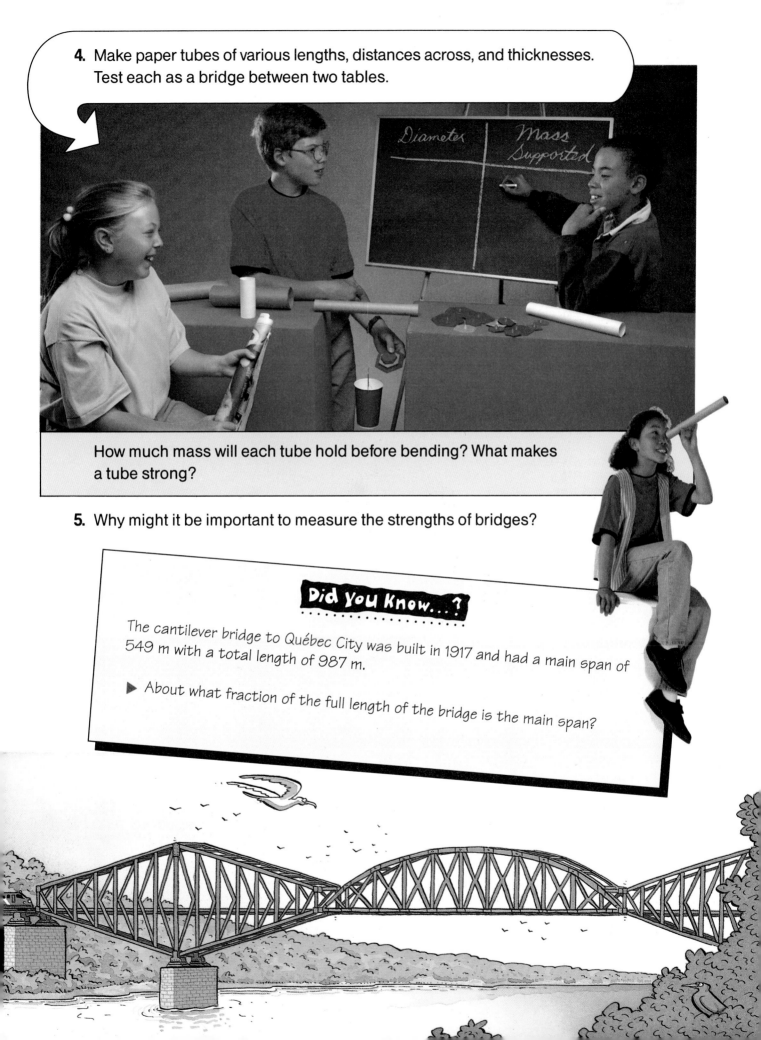

How much mass will each tube hold before bending? What makes a tube strong?

5. Why might it be important to measure the strengths of bridges?

Did You Know...?

The cantilever bridge to Québec City was built in 1917 and had a main span of 549 m with a total length of 987 m.

▶ About what fraction of the full length of the bridge is the main span?

HOW Are Simple Buildings Constructed?

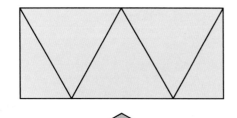

Describe the shape you expect to make, using this net.
Copy the net and make the shape.
Was your prediction right?

Work in a group.

1. Create a different net to make the same shape.

2. Describe the shape you expect to make if you connect toothpicks as shown and then connect the ends marked with the same letters.

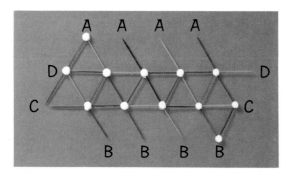

Build the shape and test your predictions.

3. Cut out 20 congruent circles like this from cardboard.
Trace the triangle on each circle.

Fold along the sides of the triangle. Punch holes at the vertices.
Start connecting the folded circles together with elastics.
What shapes do you see as you connect more and more circles?
What shape do you get with 20 circles?
Have you ever seen a structure like this? What might it be used for?

Did you know...?

These houses are built with curved rather than straight sides.

▶ What shapes do these houses remind you of?
Use nets to make models of these houses. Which has the greatest floor area?
Which do you think has the greatest volume? How can you check?

HOW Can We Model Structures?

Rosa created an interesting model for a structure. The model must be folded from a cardboard net.

Work in a group.

1. For each net, predict what the structure will look like by telling
   • how many edges and vertices or corners it has
   • how many faces and curved surfaces it has
   • how many faces or curved surfaces touch at each vertex
   • the shapes of the faces or curved surfaces that touch each other
   • something that it looks like

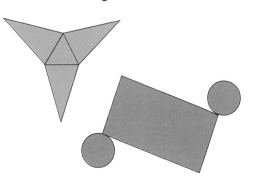

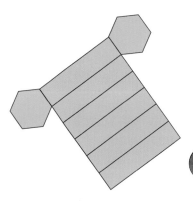

   Check your predictions by using nets to make the structures.
   Which of these shapes is a pyramid? prism? cone?

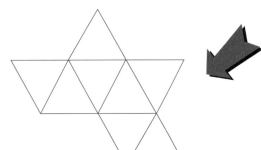

2. Make a structure from a net like this.

   Count the faces, edges, and vertices.
   Why is it easy to tell how many faces it will have from its net?
   Why is it hard to tell how many edges and vertices it will have from its net?

3. Make structures from nets like these.
How are the structures alike? different?

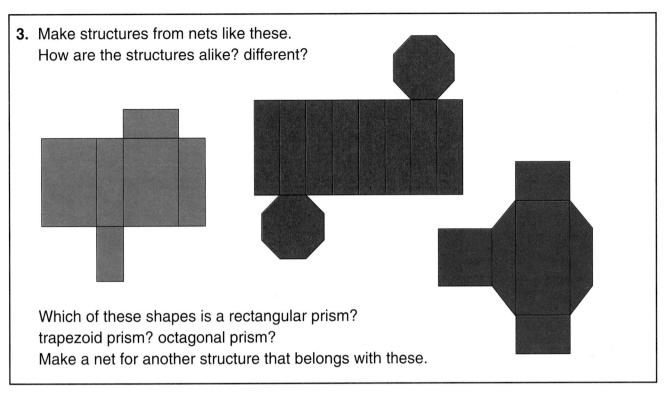

Which of these shapes is a rectangular prism?
trapezoid prism? octagonal prism?
Make a net for another structure that belongs with these.

4. Make structures from nets like these.
What type of prism are they?
How will the structures be different?
alike?

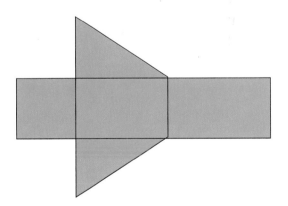

5. Is it possible to make a net for a spherical structure? Explain.

6. Create a net for a structure that you think could win the contest.
Why do you think it is a winner?

Did You Know...?

The oldest pyramid is the Djoser step pyramid in Saqqara, Egypt. It dates back to about 2630 B.C. and is about 62 m tall.

▶ How old is it?

▶ What do you think a step pyramid looks like?

▶ How many times as tall is the pyramid than you? your school?

How Can We Identify and Name the Faces of Structures?

These imprints show all the faces of one solid.

1. What solid is it?

2. What shape is each face?

   All the faces can be called **polygons**.

   > A polygon is a closed shape with three or more sides.

3. On grid or dot paper sketch
   • three different polygons.
   • three shapes that are not polygons.

Work with a partner.

Examine all the faces on the nets on pages 160 and 161.

4. Complete this chart for the number of each type of polygon found on the two pages.

	Polygon Chart number on pages 160 and 161
triangles	
rectangles	
trapezoids	
hexagons	
octagons	

5. Where did you record the number of squares? Explain why.

6. Which solids had faces which were not included in the chart? Explain why.

7. Look at these nets. Describe and name the faces.
Predict what each structure will look like.

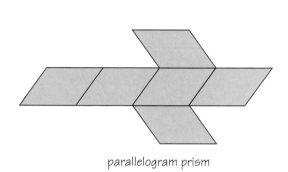

parallelogram prism

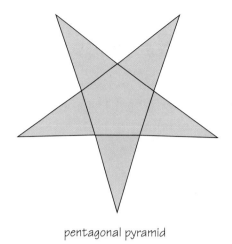

pentagonal pyramid

8. Which faces on pages 160 and 161 and in Problem 7 could also be called quadrilaterals?

9. Make up a definition and draw several examples on dot or grid paper for each type of polygon. Use descriptions such as
• number of sides   • number of vertices   • types of corner angles

triangle	rectangle	square	trapezoid
octagon	hexagon	pentagon	parallelogram

10. You can name polygons according to the number of sides. Draw two examples each for a nonagon, a decagon, and a dodecagon.

3 sides	triangle
4 sides	quadrilateral
5 sides	pentagon
6 sides	hexagon
7 sides	heptagon
8 sides	octagon
9 sides	nonagon
10 sides	decagon
12 sides	dodecagon

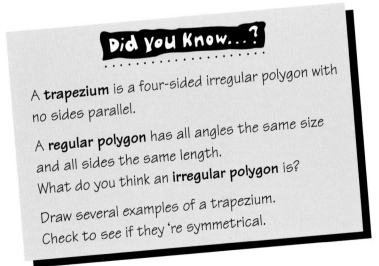

Did you Know...?

A **trapezium** is a four-sided irregular polygon with no sides parallel.

A **regular polygon** has all angles the same size and all sides the same length.
What do you think an **irregular polygon** is?

Draw several examples of a trapezium. Check to see if they're symmetrical.

? I Wonder... ?

Living Space

Find out and compare some floor areas of a variety of types of homes, such as a one-bedroom apartment, a two-storey house, or a bungalow.

Familiar Faces

Find out which shapes of faces are most commonly found on structures. Which faces are never or seldom seen?

Step Climbers

Measure the height and depth of the steps on several different staircases. Try to include a spiral staircase and some outdoor staircases. Compare the measurements.
Which staircases do you find easiest to climb?
Suggest a maximum height and depth of steps that is reasonable.

Toothpick Towers

Use toothpicks and marshmallows or peas. Build the tallest structure you can. Describe and name its faces.

Painter's Puzzle

Estimate the number of litres of paint that would be needed to paint all the walls of your classroom.

Make up your OWN investigation. Then post it on the bulletin board for others to try.

Thinking Back

Tell about a situation where each type of building information might be needed.

- height
- floor area
- mass
- volume
- age
- shape

Most building faces are polygons. Do you agree or disagree? Explain.

Write about some of the advantages and disadvantages of round homes.

What different names are there for a square?

Which name is the best one? Explain.

What else would you like to know about structures?
Tell what you would do to find out.

◀ These base ten blocks show 3.45.

Show
2.9   1.32   3.06

What would you have to add
to the blocks in the photo to
show 5?

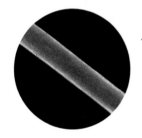

◀ This hair has
been magnified
100 times under a
microscope.

What would its actual thickness be?
Why might we look at things under
a microscope?

◀ A 24 g box of
corn flakes contains
0.6 g of fibre.
About how much
fibre would be in
this 400 g box?

▼ This animal has a fever.
Which animal might it be?
How much has its temperature risen?

Average Body Temperature (in °C)

Blue whale	35.5
Crocodile	25.6
Goat	39.9
Goldfish	23.5
Human	37.0

with Decimals

5.03

How much will it cost for 2 tapes? 4 tapes?
How many tapes could you buy with $30?

How close in length could a king cobra and a paradise tree snake be?
How far apart in length could they be?

paradise tree snake — 0.9 m to 1.2 m   king cobra snake — 3.7 m to 5.5 m

What might you be able
to do in 0.1 of an hour?
0.01 of an hour?

When might
you have to add
or subtract
decimal numbers?

167

In what ways is a circle like a square?

$1.98 $2.39   79¢ $1.49   85¢

Ron is finding the cost of a journal and a pencil case.

$2 + 85¢ is $2.85. Then take away 2¢.

Explain his thinking.

```
  1.98
+ 0.85
------
  2.83
```

Susan is finding how much more Duo-Tangs cost than looseleaf paper.

$2.39 − $1.39 is $1

Finish her work.

```
  2.39
− 1.49
```

1. What is the cost of a journal and Duo-Tangs?

2. How much more do Duo-Tangs cost than a report cover?

Work with a partner.

Use play money. Record addition or subtraction sentences.

3. What is the cost of looseleaf paper and a report cover? What is the difference in their costs?

4. How many different items can you buy with $5? What change would you receive?

5. Find an item that costs about $1.50 more than another item. Exactly how much more is it?

6. Why do you think that many prices end in 9? Does this make adding and subtracting prices easy or hard? Explain.

When you find $\frac{1}{2}$, $\frac{1}{3}$, or $\frac{1}{5}$ of a number, the part is a whole number. What could the number be?

Mixing Drinks

1.36 L   0.35 L

Can these drinks be mixed in a 1.5 L container?

Margot estimates.

```
 1.36  is almost 1.4
+0.35  is almost 0.4
              1.8    Too much
```

Why does she write this?

Now she is calculating exactly how much she will have.

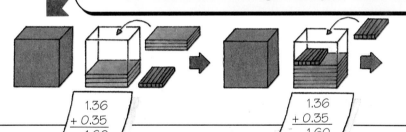

```
 1.36
+0.35
 1.60
```

```
 1.36
+0.35
 1.60
 0.11
```

Why did she add 3 flats?
5 longs?
Finish her work.

Elan is mixing 1.14 L of apple juice and 0.29 L of cranberry juice.

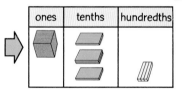

1. Estimate to see if he can use a 1.5 L container.

Elan is calculating exactly how much he will have.

ones	tenths	hundredths

ones	tenths	hundredths

What trade did he make? Why? What will he do next? Finish his work.

```
  1
 1.14
+0.29
   3
```

Work in a group.

Estimate and then calculate. Model your solutions.

1.36 L   0.95 L   1.89 L   1.5 L   2.84 L   0.75 L   0.95 L   1.14 L   1.36 L

2. What is the least amount you can get mixing 2 of the drinks? 3 of them?

3. What is the greatest amount you can get mixing 2 of the drinks? 3 of them?

4. Can all of the drinks be mixed in a 12 L container? Explain.

What is the area of this shape?
Make 2 other shapes with 8 pegs touching
the elastics and 2 pegs inside.
Find the areas. What do you notice?

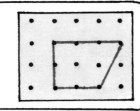

Single Luge Results

	1988	1992
Men's	3:05.54	3:02.36
Women's	3:03.97	3:06.69

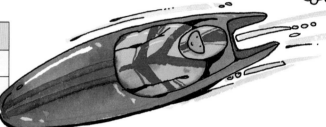

3:05.54 is read
three minutes, five and fifty-four hundredths seconds.
Read the other times.

Natalia estimates how many seconds
faster the men's time was in 1992
than in 1988.

```
  5.5 is almost            6
– 2.3 is a bit more than 2
              almost 4
```

Why does she write this?
Why does she ignore the 3 min?

Then she calculates.

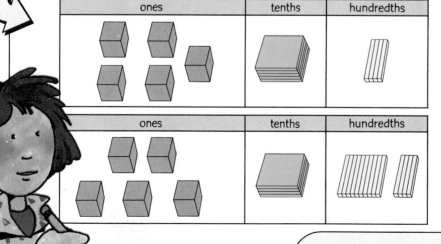

```
  414
 5.5̷4
– 2.36
     8
```

What trade did she make? Why?
What will she do next? Finish her work.

170

1. In which year was the women's time faster?

Estimate how many seconds faster.

Roberto is calculating how much faster by counting on.

3.97 to 4.00 is 0.03

4.00 to 6.00 is 2.0

6.00 to 6.69 is

Finish his work.

Work in a group.

Estimate and then use different methods to subtract. Model your solutions.

2. In which year was the women's single luge time faster than the men's? How much faster?

3. In which year was the time faster for each skiing event? How much faster?

Alpine Skiing Results

	1988	1992
Men's downhill	1:59.63	1:50.37
Men's slalom	1:39.47	1:44.39
Women's downhill	1:25.86	1:52.55
Women's giant slalom	2:06.49	2:12.74

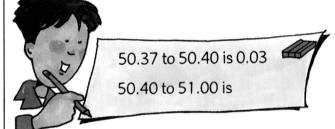

50.37 to 50.40 is 0.03

50.40 to 51.00 is

4. In which swimming event were the men's and women's winning times the closest? How close were they?

5. Why do you think decimal places to the hundredths are used to record times? How do you think officials decide how accurate to be?

1992 Swimming Results

	Men's	Women's
100 m freestyle	0:49.02	0:54.64
100 m backstroke	0:53.98	1:00.68
100 m breast stroke	1:01.50	1:08.00
100 m butterfly	0:53.52	0:58.62

Take Your Pick

0 TO 6

Use each digit from 0 to 6 once to make this true.

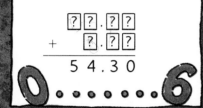

$$\begin{array}{r} \boxed{?}\,\boxed{?}\,.\,\boxed{?}\,\boxed{?} \\ +\quad \boxed{?}\,.\,\boxed{?}\,\boxed{?} \\ \hline 5\;4\;.\;3\;0 \end{array}$$

PREDICTIONS

Predict the numbers that will be in the seventh row.

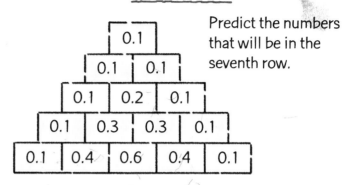

```
            0.1
         0.1    0.1
      0.1    0.2    0.1
   0.1    0.3    0.3    0.1
0.1    0.4    0.6    0.4    0.1
```

SUM AND DIFFERENCE

Luis and Elena are combining their money to buy a gift.
They have a total of $52.08.
Elena had $12.08 more than Luis.
How much did each of them have before combining their money?

MISSING TOTALS

$35.78 was spent in 4 stores.

SCIENCE +

Jerry's

Fortune

Sam's

$ 7.20 Thank you!

Total 9.11

How much might have been spent at each of Science + and Sam's?

BUYING BULK

What is the difference between the highest price and the lowest price?

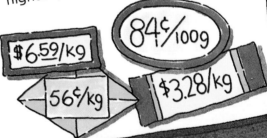

$6.59/kg

84¢/100g

56¢/kg

$3.28/kg

Make up other problems. Post them on the bulletin board for your classmates to solve.

Arrange 6 counters in 3 straight lines of 3 each.

Growing Bigger

Multiplying by powers of ten

. . . she opened it, and found in it a very small cake, on which the words "EAT ME" were beautifully marked in currants . . . So she set to work, and very soon finished off the cake. . . . "Curiouser and curiouser!" cried Alice . . . "Now I'm opening out like the largest telescope that ever was! Goodbye, feet!"

from *Alice in Wonderland* by Lewis Carroll

height 1.4 m

— nose width 3.2 cm

arm length (not including hand) 3.8 dm

finger length 6.4 cm

thumb width 1.4 cm

Suppose each part of Alice became 10 times as long and 10 times as wide. How wide would her thumb be?

Decimetres are 10 times centimetres. So Alice's thumb would be 1.4 dm wide.

So Alice's thumb would be 14 cm wide.

10×1.0

10×0.4

Work with a partner.

Who is right? Explain.

1. What would be Alice's new finger length? nose width? arm length? height?

2. Find each other's
   · height   · finger length   · thumb width   · arm length
   What would these measurements be if you ate the cake?

3. Suppose the cake made Alice 100 times as tall and wide. What would be her new finger length? nose width? arm length? height?
   How do these answers relate to those from Problem 1?

4.

The digit from the tenths place is in the ones place after you multiply by 10.

$10 \times 4.2 = 42.0$

Explain. Which digit would be in the ones place after you multiply by 100?

When a number cube is rolled
- an even number occurs about $\frac{2}{3}$ of the time
- a number greater than 10 occurs about $\frac{1}{6}$ of the time

The cube has 3 pairs of numbers each with a sum of 14.
What numbers could be on the cube?

Buying Foreign Money

About how much does it cost to buy $5 U.S.?

Tara estimates.

$5 \times \$1 = \$5$ and
$5 \times 25¢ = 5$ quarters

Cost in Canadian Dollars, December 24, 1992	
1 U.S. dollar	$1.26
1 British pound	$1.92
1 German mark	$0.79
1 Japanese yen	$0.01
1 French franc	$0.23
1 Irish punt	$2.09
1 Argentine peso	$1.30

Alan estimates.

$5 \times \$1 = \$5$ and
$5 \times 30¢ = 5 \times 3$ dimes
$= 15$ dimes

Why did Tara use 5 quarters?
Why did Alan use 5 groups of 3 dimes?
Finish each student's work.

1. About how much would 5 British pounds cost? 5 French francs?

2. Of which currency is Vera estimating the cost of 5 units?

3. What is the cost of $10 US? 10 British pounds? 10 German marks?

174

Use play money.

4. A French franc has almost the same value as one quarter. How can you use this fact to estimate the cost of 12 francs? 25 francs? 48 francs? 58 francs? Which costs were easy to estimate? Explain why.

5. About how much Canadian money will each item cost?

6. Why is it useful to be able to estimate the cost in Canadian dollars of items in foreign money?

7. Make up foreign money problems.
8×0.23 11×1.92 17×1.30

8. About how much Canadian money is each U.S. coin worth?

9. Foreign money exchange rates change daily. The cost of $1 U.S. was as low as $1.14 and as high as $1.29 within one year's time. Find the current exchange rates in the financial section of a newspaper.
Estimate the cost of buying 50 units of money of a country you might like to visit.

A plane leaves Toronto at 5:20 p.m. and arrives at Calgary at 7:35 p.m. (Calgary time). How long did the flight take?

Comparing Masses of Small Animals

Choosing a multiplication algorithm

The royal antelope is the smallest antelope.
Its mass is about 3.3 kg.
At what age might a human have that mass?

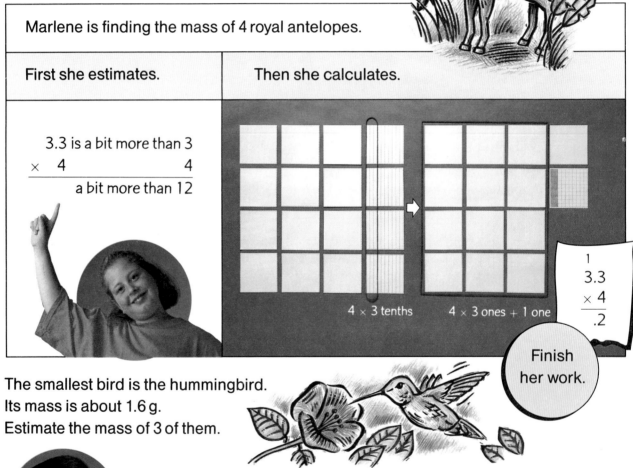

Marlene is finding the mass of 4 royal antelopes.

First she estimates.	Then she calculates.

3.3 is a bit more than 3
× 4   4
a bit more than 12

4 × 3 tenths   4 × 3 ones + 1 one

```
   1
  3.3
 ×  4
 ────
   .2
```

Finish her work.

The smallest bird is the hummingbird.
Its mass is about 1.6 g.
Estimate the mass of 3 of them.

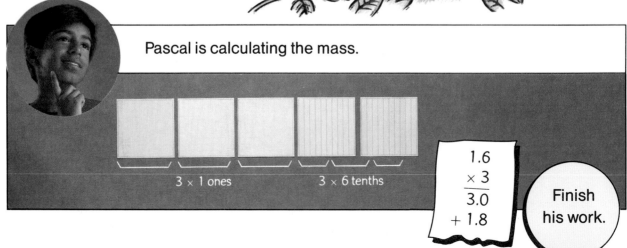

Pascal is calculating the mass.

3 × 1 ones   3 × 6 tenths

```
  1.6
 ×  3
 ────
  3.0
+ 1.8
```

Finish his work.

176

The smallest marsupial is the long-tailed planigale. Its mass is 4.21 g.

1. What is the mass of 2 long-tailed planigales? Estimate and then calculate the mass of 5 of them. How close was your estimate? Show two ways to find the mass of 8 long-tailed planigales.

Work in a group.

Estimate and then calculate. Model your solutions. Use this information.

Smallest Animals

bumblebee bat	1.87 g
northern pygmy mouse	7.5 g
miniature chihuahua	0.63 kg
Netherland dwarf rabbit	1.02 kg
palmate newt	2.39 g

2. For which animal is Cheryl finding the mass of 3 of them? How do you know?

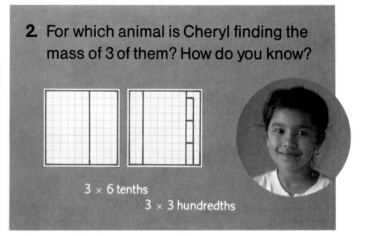

3 × 6 tenths
3 × 3 hundredths

3. What is the mass of each group of animals? Use your calculator to check.

Rabbits   Chihuahuas   Mice   Newts   Bats

4. Which is heavier— 1 bumblebee bat or 3 miniature chihuahuas? Explain.

5. Which way should each of the balance scales tilt?

6. Why do you think there was no data given about the smallest insects?

There are lots of ways to calculate 2.56×8.
Here are some. Can you think of any more?

1. You could show 2.56 eight times using decimal grids.

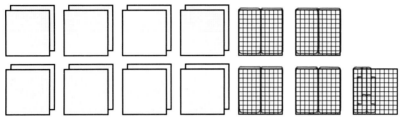

8×2 ones
$= 16$ ones

8×5 tenths
$= 40$ tenths
$= 4.0$ ones

8×6 hundredths
$= 48$ hundredths

$8 \times 2.56 = 20.48$

2. You might model with money.

8×2 dollars $= 16$ dollars   \$16.00
8×5 dimes $= 40$ dimes   4.00
8×6 pennies $= 48$ pennies   0.48
                              \$20.48

$8 \times 2.56 = 20.48$

3. You could double 3 times.

$2 \times 2.56 = 5.12$
$2 \times 5.12 = 10.24$
$2 \times 10.24 = 20.48$

$8 \times 2.56 = 20.48$

4. You might multiply 8 and 256 hundredths.

$$
\begin{array}{r}
256 \text{ hundredths} \\
\times \quad 8 \\
\hline
2048 \text{ hundredths} = 20.48
\end{array}
$$

$8 \times 2.56 = 20.48$

Work in a group.

Show two different ways to do each multiplication.

1. $\begin{array}{r} 3.14 \\ \times \quad 8 \\ \hline \end{array}$ **2.** $\begin{array}{r} 5.6 \\ \times \quad 11 \\ \hline \end{array}$ **3.** $\begin{array}{r} 1.35 \\ \times \quad 4 \\ \hline \end{array}$

4. 5×3.32 **5.** 6×1.38 **6.** 9×0.25

DOZEN

12 pens cost exactly $12. How many of each pen were bought?

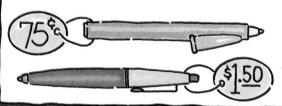

PATTERNS

Find the next three numbers in each pattern.

0.23, 2.3, 23.0, . . .
3.45, 6.90, 13.80, . . .
13.4, 26.8, 40.2, . . .

EARTHQUAKES

The Richter scale is used to measure earthquakes.
The higher the number, the stronger the earthquake.
A difference of 1.0 means an earthquake that is 10 times as strong.
A difference of 2.0 means an earthquake that is 100 times as strong.

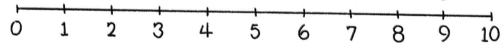

How many times as strong an earthquake is 4.6 as 3.6? 7.2 as 4.2?
What earthquake would be 1000 times as strong as 3.8?

HOW MANY?

How many of each ticket could you buy with $50?
What change would you get?

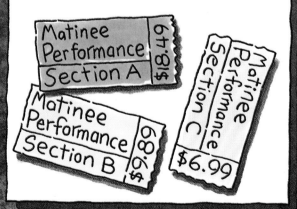

Matinee Performance Section A $8.49
Matinee Performance Section B $4.89
Matinee Performance Section C $6.99

FILL IN

Fill in the digits to make this true.

$$\begin{array}{r} 2.\boxed{?} \\ \times 5 \\ \hline \boxed{?}1.5 \end{array}$$

Make up other problems. Post them on the bulletin board for your classmates to solve.

Find 10 ways to express 97. Use any combination of addition, subtraction, multiplication, or division.

Getting Money Back

Dividing by powers of ten

SALE
GET BACK $\frac{1}{10}$ OF PRICE

How much money would you get back from a $10 purchase? a $1 purchase? a 10¢ purchase?

How much money is paid? given back?

Explain why this amount is given back.

PAY   GET BACK

1. Conrad spent $56.80. How many $1 coins does he get back? how many dimes? pennies?
   Why might you calculate 56.80 ÷ 10 to find $\frac{1}{10}$ of 56.80?

Work with a partner.

Use play money. Write division sentences.

2. How much money would you get back from a $35.90 purchase?
   Why do the amounts paid and given back have the same digits?
   Why is the ones digit in the amount paid the same as the tenths digit in the amount given back?

3. How much would you get back from each purchase to the nearest cent?

$132·70
$48·25
$30
$235·78

4. What fraction is given back here?
   What number would you divide by?
   How much would you get back from these purchases?

$200 $340 $527·20

GET $1·00 BACK ON EVERY $100 SPENT

5. What digit in the amount given back is the same as the hundreds digit in the amount paid? Explain.
   What about the tens digit in the amount paid?

6. How are dividing by 10 and 100 alike? different?

7. How does knowing how to multiply by 10 help you to divide by 10?

180

If this shape is 1, what might $\frac{1}{5}$ look like? $\frac{3}{5}$?

Estimating Areas of Garbage Zones

Granby, PQ has an area of 72.6 km². If the city is divided into 5 zones for garbage pick up, estimate the average area of each zone.

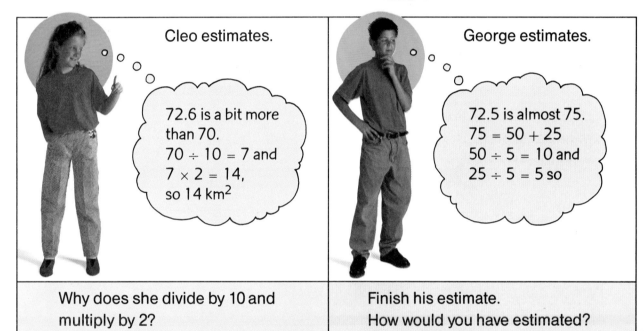

Cleo estimates.

> 72.6 is a bit more than 70.
> 70 ÷ 10 = 7 and
> 7 × 2 = 14,
> so 14 km²

George estimates.

> 72.5 is almost 75.
> 75 = 50 + 25
> 50 ÷ 5 = 10 and
> 25 ÷ 5 = 5 so

Why does she divide by 10 and multiply by 2?	Finish his estimate. How would you have estimated?

Work with a partner.

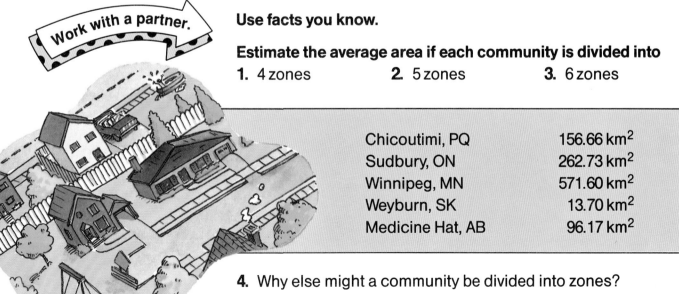

Use facts you know.

Estimate the average area if each community is divided into

1. 4 zones   **2.** 5 zones   **3.** 6 zones

Chicoutimi, PQ	156.66 km²
Sudbury, ON	262.73 km²
Winnipeg, MN	571.60 km²
Weyburn, SK	13.70 km²
Medicine Hat, AB	96.17 km²

4. Why else might a community be divided into zones?
Do you think that zones usually have the same area?

181

Date	High Temperature	Low Temperature
Jan. 20	0° C	−5° C
Jan. 21	2° C	−4° C
Jan. 22	−1° C	−5° C

What is the difference between the high and low temperatures each day?

Finding the Price

4L of milk cost $3.79
What is the price of 1 L?

Chris finds the price of 1 L.

First he estimates.

3.79 is almost 4.
4 ÷ 4 = 1, so less than $1

Then he calculates.

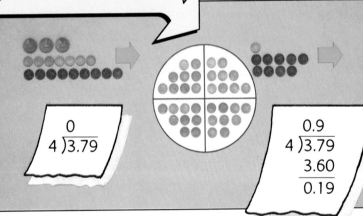

$$4\overline{)3.79} \quad \begin{array}{r} 0 \end{array}$$

$$\begin{array}{r} 0.9 \\ 4\overline{)3.79} \\ 3.60 \\ \hline 0.19 \end{array}$$

What trade did he make?
What trade will he make next?
Finish his work.

What could you do with the remainder?

A set of three mixing bowls costs $5.19.
Estimate the average price of one bowl.

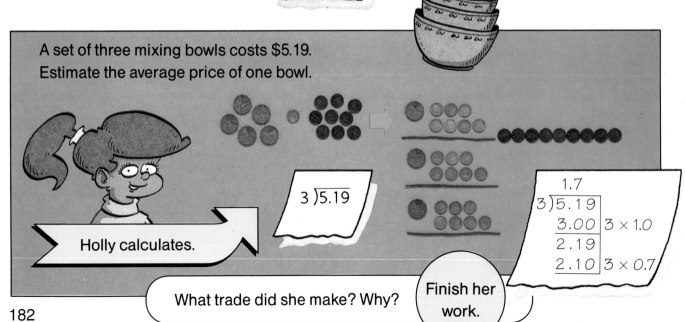

$$3\overline{)5.19}$$

$$\begin{array}{r} 1.7 \\ 3\overline{)5.19} \\ 3.00 \\ \hline 2.19 \\ 2.10 \end{array} \begin{array}{l} 3 \times 1.0 \\ \\ 3 \times 0.7 \end{array}$$

Holly calculates.

What trade did she make? Why?

Finish her work.

1. Would you get the same price as Chris for 1 L of milk if you did what Ann says? Explain.

We found these prices before. We changed dollars and cents to cents before we divided.

Work in a group.

Estimate and then calculate to the nearest cent.
Model your solutions.

2. These CDs are on sale for $\frac{1}{2}$ the prices shown. What is each sale price?

THE DECIMAL POINTS. $18.95
$22.49
THE DIVIDERS
ELVIS AND THE SUBTRACTIONS $19.95

3. What is the price for 1 of each different item?

KID-TALK
6 ISSUES PER YEAR FOR $13.98
YOUNG FOLKS' ENCYCLOPEDIA $14.95 A SET
10 TARTS FOR $3.29
8 ORANGES FOR $2.59

4. Find the price.
   - 1 wrench from a set of 7 for $24.99
   - 1 tape in a set of 5 for $46.40
   - 1 game in a box of 5 for $66.20

5. Visit a store and compare the prices of
   - different sizes of the same brand
   - the same sizes of different brands

Dividing

There are lots of ways to calculate 7.38 ÷ 6. Here are some. Can you think of any more?

1. You might use base ten blocks and share among 6.

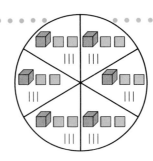

7.38 ÷ 6 = 1.23

2. You could show 7.38 on decimal grids and divide into groups of 6.

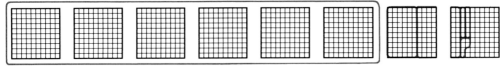

1 group of 6 ones   2 groups of 6 tenths   3 groups of 6 hundredths

1.23   7.38 ÷ 6 = 1.23

3. You might rename as hundredths and rename again as numbers easy to divide by 6.

7.38 = 738 hundredths
     = 600 hundredths + 120 hundredths + 18 hundredths

600 hundredths ÷ 6 = 100 hundredths

120 hundredths ÷ 6 = 20 hundredths

18 hundredths ÷ 6 = $\dfrac{3 \text{ hundredths}}{123 \text{ hundredths}}$ = 1.23

7.38 ÷ 6 = 1.23

4. You could arrange play money into equal groups of 6.

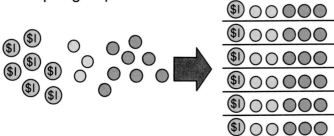

7.38 ÷ 6 = 1.23

Work in a group.

Show two different ways to do each division.

1. $9\overline{)8.88}$ **2.** $3\overline{)32.49}$

3. $7\overline{)81.6}$ **4.** 22.4 ÷ 4

5. 32.1 ÷ 5   **6.** 7.25 ÷ 8

Take Your Pick

PENCILS

Choose 3 pencils.
Measure each to the nearest tenth of a centimetre.
Add the 3 lengths and divide by 3.
What do you think this length is called?

SHARING LAND

Four cousins are sharing this rectangle of land.

2 km

3.45 km

About how many square kilometres of land will each cousin get?

COST OF EATING

It costs, on average, $135.45 each week to feed a family of four. About how much does it cost each day to feed the family? each family member?

MOVING DIGITS

Use 2, 3, 4, 5, and 6 in different positions.

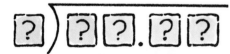

What is the greatest possible quotient? the least?
How can you get a quotient of exactly 5.89?

KEEP DIVIDING

You divide a number by 2.
You divide that quotient by 2.
You divide the last quotient by 2.
The result is 1.26.
What was the original number?

Make up other problems. Post them on the bulletin board for your classmates to solve.

Solving a Problem by Solving a Simpler Problem

Try this problem before going on.

MIDDLE NUMBER

The middle number of 3 numbers is 9.16. What will the middle number be if each number is doubled?

Ginette's group solved the problem by solving a simpler problem.

We used 3 numbers whose middle number was easy to find.

| Numbers | 1 | 2 | 3 | → | Middle Number | 2 |
| Doubled | 2 | 4 | 6 | → | Middle Number | 4 |

It looks like the middle number is doubled too.

We checked with 3 other easy numbers.

| Numbers | 5 | 6 | 7 | → | Middle Number | 6 | |
| Doubled | 10 | 12 | 14 | → | Middle Number | 12 | doubled |

The new middle number would be 2 × 9.16 or 18.32.

What if the numbers were tripled?

Work in a group.

Solve each problem by solving a simpler problem.

AVERAGE RAINFALL

The average monthly rainfall for 6 months was 28.5 mm. If it had rained 1 mm more each month, what would the average have been?

HOW MANY DIGITS?

How many digits would be in the product of 999 × 999?

ODD LENGTHS

How much string is needed to cut lengths of 0.1 m, 0.3 m, 0.5 m, 0.7 m, 0.9 m, 1.1 m, 1.3 m, 1.5 m, 1.7 m, 1.9 m, 2.1 m, 2.3 m, 2.5 m, 2.7 m, 2.9 m?

Practising What You've Learned

Write a problem for each of these. Then solve.

1. 7.2 − 1.75

2. 5 × 1.46

3. 25.7 ÷ 10

4. 6) 42.24

Solve.

CANADA 48¢

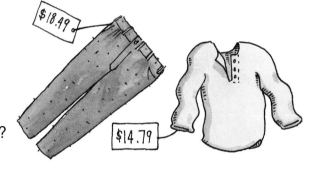

$18.49

$14.79

5. How much would 10 stamps cost?

6. How much do the pants and shirt cost together? How much more do the pants cost than the shirt?

7. About how many plants could you buy with $40?

$6.29 EACH

8. 1.85 L of oil is mixed with 4.2 L of gasoline. How much of the mixture is there?

9. Add these jump heights.
1.53 m   1.68 m   1.81 m

10. The largest camera lens is about 1.37 m across. The smallest camera lens, other than for surgery and spying, is 2.9 cm across. How many more metres across is the large lens than the small one?
About how many small lenses would fit across the large lens?

11. About 0.68 of Canadian households own a microwave oven. About how many households would you expect to own a microwave oven in a town of 5000 households?

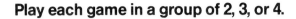
Playing Games for Practice

Play each game in a group of 2, 3, or 4.

Target 2.1

- Roll a die 2 times to get a 2-digit number. Use the digits in the order rolled as the ones digit and the tenths digit.
- Repeat 2 more times.
- Add or subtract any 2 of your 3 numbers trying to get as close as possible to 2.1.
- Your score is how far you are from 2.1.
- Take turns. Play 5 rounds.
- The player with the lowest score wins.

Example

3.2   5.4   1.2

Using 3.2 and 1.2, 3.2 − 1.2 = 2.0.
Score 0.1 since 2.1 − 2.0 = 0.1.

Estimate 500

- Roll a die 3 times to get a 3-digit number. Use the digits in the order rolled as the ones digit, the tenths digit, and the hundredths digit.
- Enter your number on a calculator.
- Estimate what number to multiply it by to get as close as possible to 500. Then calculate.
- Take turns. The player with the closest estimate scores a point.
- The first player to score 10 points wins.

Example

3.65

Estimate   Multiply by 130, 4 × 130 = 520

Answer   474.5

HOW LIKELY?

If you spin the spinner twice, what is the probability of the sum being greater than 10? the difference being greater than 3?

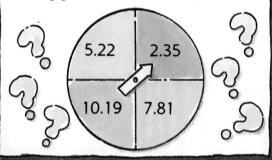

ARRANGING DIGITS

Create a decimal number and a 1-digit whole number.
Arrange the digits to get
- the greatest quotient
- the least quotient

TRACK RECORD

Donovan Bailey's winning time for the 100 m dash in the 1996 Olympics was 9.84 s. What would you expect the winning times to be for these distances?

200 m   400 m   800 m

Look up the records to check your predictions.

BUYING SPREE

Mike spent $28.03. What did he buy?

MYSTERY NUMBERS

If you divide a number by 4, the quotient is 1.81. What would the quotient be if you divide the number by 2? What is the number?

Make up other problems. Post them on the bulletin board for your classmates to solve.

1. Write an addition, a subtraction, a multiplication, and a division sentence with this answer.

2. Tell how you could use a measuring tape to multiply 6 by 1.25.

3. Order from least to greatest without actually calculating. Tell how you did it.

   $5 + 4.52$ $5 - 4.52$ 5×4.52 $5\overline{)4.52}$

4. You multiply a number by 5 and the product is about 3. What do you know about the number?

5. How and why are the answers to these related?
   5×342 5×34.2 5×3.42

6. Estimate the quotient of 34.16 and 7. Then calculate.

7. Find two lengths that differ by 2 cm and total 6.42 cm.

8. How much is the change each time?
   $2.43 from $5
   $8.82 from $10

9. Find the perimeter of this rectangle.

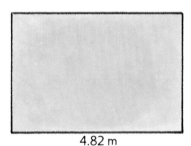

3.42 m

4.82 m

10. Four friends are sharing this giant licorice. How much does each get? How much more would each get if the licorice was 1 m longer?

3.44 m

190

Thinking Back

Is multiplying by 0.1 the same as dividing by 10? Why or why not?

Which operation — addition, subtraction, multiplication, or division — do you find easiest with decimals? Tell why.

Could 4.2 be the difference of two numbers with digits in the hundredths places? Explain.

Is this sum correct? Explain.

```
  3.45
+ 1.2
------
  3.57
```

How are dividing decimals and dividing whole numbers alike? different?

What questions do you still have about calculating with decimals?

UNIT 11 Examining Symmetry

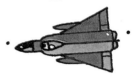

▼ Find the mistakes in the reflection.

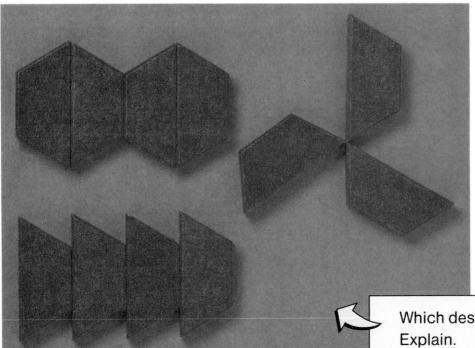

◄ Tell which design was made by sliding, flipping, or turning a trapezoid pattern block.

Which designs show symmetry? Explain.

and Motion Geometry

▼ Use any pattern block except the trapezoid. Make a design that suggests you are sliding it. Does your design suggest any other motions?

▲ How are the cards alike? different?

▼ Is this octagon symmetrical? Explain. Create a different octagon that is not symmetrical. Explain why it isn't.

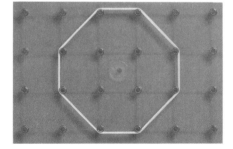

Write the word NOON on a piece of paper. Turn the paper upside down. What do you notice? The same thing happens to a code word for help. What is the code word?

Examine patterns on your clothing and the clothing of students around you. Do any patterns suggest slides, flips, or turns?

Explain Paul's thinking.

$$11 \times 34 = 340 + 34$$
$$= 374$$

Use Paul's method to multiply 11×57 and 11×302.

Coding and Decoding Messages

Use a Mira to decode this message.

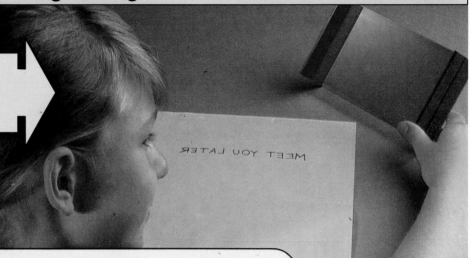

Where did you place your Mira?

The Mira locates the **flip line**.
The decoded message is the **flip image** of the coded message.

1. Find the flip image of each coded message. Is each flip line horizontal or vertical?

2. How might a Mira have been used to code the messages?
   Code this message.

   WAIT FOR ME

SOCCER AT 5

WE GOT A DOG

I HOPE SHE PICKS ME

LET'S TALK

3. Count the squares from the flip line to the
   • coded T   • decoded T
   • coded Y   • decoded Y

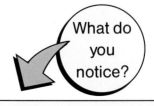

What do you notice?

| Y | S | A | E | | S | I | | S | I | H | T | | T | H | I | S | | I | S | | E | A | S | Y |

4. Write this message on a grid.

STOP NOW

Flip it to code it.
Count the squares from the flip line to the first and
last letters in the original message.
Predict these distances for the coded message.
Check your predictions.

5. When you flip a message,
  • do any of the letters change size?
  • does the distance between
    the letters change?
Explain.

6. Which letters in these coded messages
appear as usual? Decode the messages.

MATH FIRST

FRENCH NEXT

7. Where do you place a Mira so that each letter appears as usual when coded?

A B C D E H I L M O S T Y

8. Write this message.

DOUBLE FLIP

Flip it horizontally to code it.
Then flip the coded message vertically.
What do you notice?

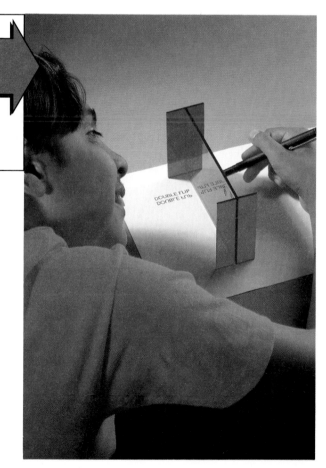

9. Code a message by flipping.
Give it to another group to decode.

10. June sent this message to her mom
before her mom left on a trip.
Use a Mira to decode it.
You need to place your Mira
differently for each letter.

These lines are parallel.
Draw one line parallel to another.
Tell how you did it.
Could you do it another way? If so, how?

Changing Appearances

Broken sunglasses

With your book right side up,
you are viewing the picture
The tail of a fish.
Do you agree with the title?

Time to turn the hourglass over

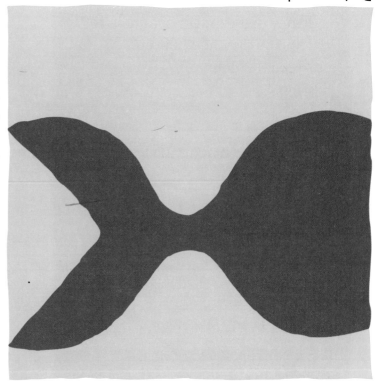

A diving mermaid

The tail of a fish

from *The turn about, think about, look about book*
by Beau Gardner

1. Turn your book
$\frac{1}{4}$ turn clockwise.

Which picture
are you viewing now?

Turn your book another $\frac{1}{4}$ turn clockwise.
Which picture are you viewing now?
Describe how you are holding your book.

Turn your book another $\frac{1}{4}$ turn clockwise.
Which picture are you viewing?

2. What single turn from right side up lets you view *Broken sunglasses*?

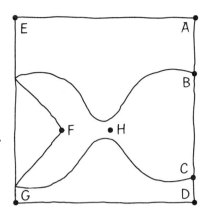

3. Trace the picture from the previous page. Label the points A to H.

4. Use A as a turn centre.
Hold your tracing down at A.
Turn your tracing $\frac{1}{4}$ turn clockwise.
What direction is the tail pointing?
Which picture is this?
Return your tracing to right side up.

5. Repeat Problem 4 for a $\frac{1}{4}$ turn clockwise at each turn centre B to H.
What did you notice about the direction of the tail?
Which turn centre moves the picture farthest to the right? to the left? up? down?

6. How far do you have to turn the picture counterclockwise to have it end up the same as a $\frac{1}{4}$ turn clockwise?

7. Why would a picture like this not be as interesting when making $\frac{1}{4}$ turns?

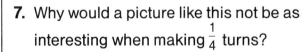

8. Create a picture that looks like something different when you turn it. Describe the amount of turn to make it look different.

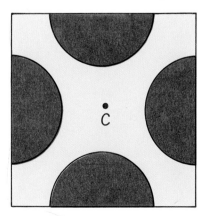

197

The area of one face of a cube is
1 square unit.

What is the area of all the faces of
the cube?

Capturing Treasure

Examining slides

Celine is close to capturing the treasure.
She can use these keys or the mouse.

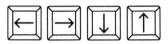

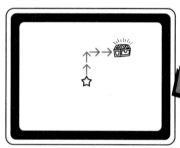

What two moves with the arrow keys
will get her the treasure? Does the
order of pressing the keys matter?

A single move, or slide, of the mouse ↗
would also get her the treasure.

1. Compare the direction of this slide to
the slide above. What about the
lengths of the slide arrows?

Use grid paper.

2. Show each move with a counter. Put a dot
in the centre of each start and end square.
Then draw each slide arrow as if the
mouse was used.

2 ↑ , 1 →	3 ↑ , 2 →	4 ↑ , 2 →
3 ↑ , 2 ←	9 ↑ , 6 →	6 ↑ , 4 ←

Which slide arrows are in the same general
direction? in the exact same direction?
the same length?

3. You might describe this slide as very
gradual up to the right.

How might you describe these slides?

How many rectangles are in each figure?

Predicting Garden Patterns   Predicting and justifying pattern extensions

Marc drew a series of diagrams to show how a square garden could be divided into smaller plots.

How many plots are in each diagram?
How many will the next diagram show?
Use the number pattern to decide how many diagrams are needed to show more than 1000 plots.

Work with a partner.

What fraction of the whole garden is each plot?

1.   **2.**   **3.**

Draw diagrams using dot paper.

4. How many plots will the next two diagrams in the series show?
Use the number pattern to decide how many diagrams are needed to show more than 50 plots.

5. Make a series of at least three diagrams for dividing a garden of a different shape into smaller plots.
Estimate at each step what fraction of the whole garden each plot is.

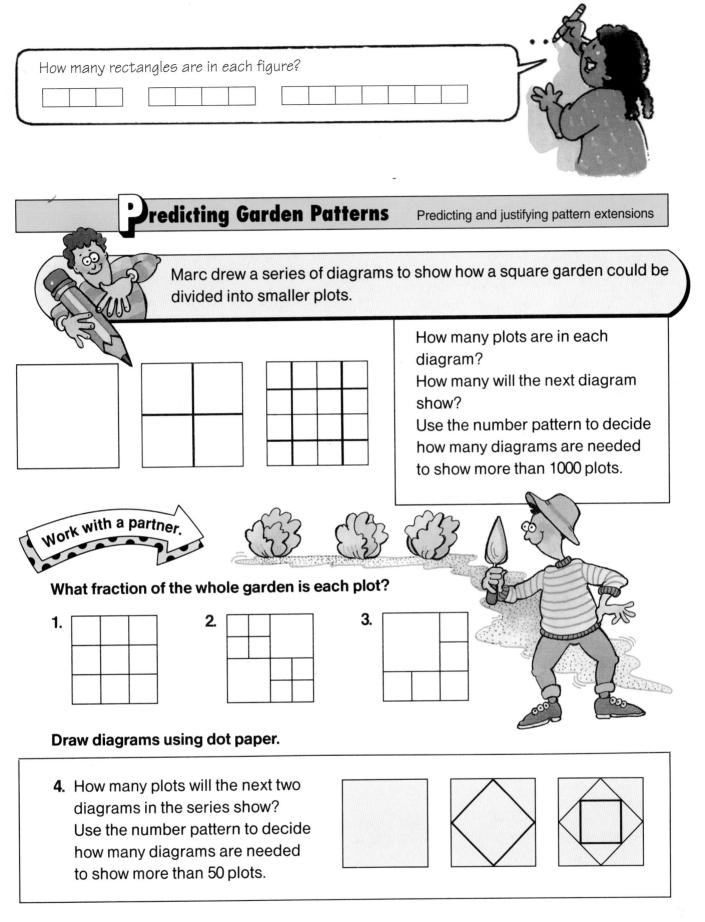

199

Place decimal points in each number so that the answers are about $50.

$992 − $491 − $11 $4225 + $155 − $712

$9992 − $199 − $3412

Exploring the Environment   Recognizing tessellations created with regular and irregular shapes

1. How are these tessellations or tiling patterns the same? different? Which patterns use regular shapes? irregular shapes? Explain what you mean by regular and irregular.

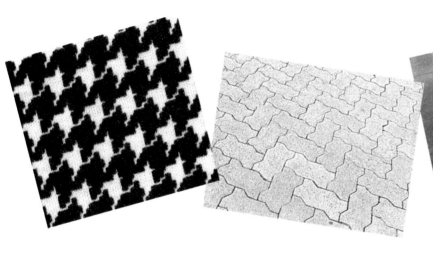

2. Are there any gaps in this floor pattern? Where do the shapes overlap?

3. How many different shapes are used in this quilt pattern? Model it.

4. Artists made these 3 patterns for fabrics and wrapping paper. Describe the shapes in each pattern.

   Trace one of the shapes.

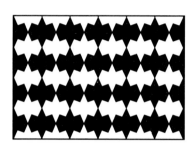  

5. This a honeycomb. Why do you think we can call it a tessellation?

6. This is a geodesic dome. What is the basic shape the architect used?

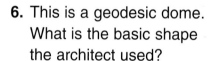

7. Tell where you have seen tiling patterns with regular and irregular shapes in your home or neighborhood.

8. Do you prefer tessellations made with regular or irregular shapes? Why?

Which do you think is closest to 5000? Explain.

499 × 10   99 × 50
500 × 9   25 × 19

Making Counter Top Designs

Covering surfaces with tessellating shapes

Use pattern blocks.

1. Jessica chose the hexagon and modelled the counter top.
   Are there other tiling patterns or tessellations she could make with the hexagons?

2. Choose another pattern block shape. Make a counter top using that shape. Tell why you chose your shape.

3. Cleo chose the triangle. Model what her counter top looks like.
   Are there other tiling patterns she could make with the triangles?

4. Jessica found another shape in Cleo's triangle pattern. Which shape do you think she saw?

5. Make a tiling pattern using a different pattern block shape. Describe any other shapes you see in your pattern.

6. Use dot paper to record your tessellation. Use color to show the pattern. Ask your partner to describe your design.

7. Tell your partner how to make this pattern with blocks. Try using the words *flip, slide,* or *turn*.

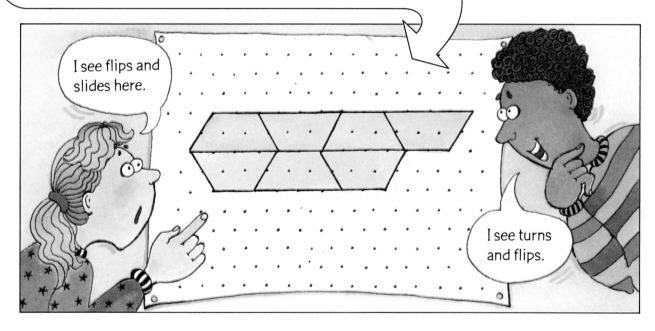

I see flips and slides here.

I see turns and flips.

8. Draw another tessellation on dot paper. Use the words *slide, flip,* or *turn* to help your partner make the pattern with blocks.

9. Use pattern blocks to tessellate an area that is at least 25 cm by 25 cm.

10. Investigate if it is possible to tessellate using only
  • the blue rhombus and slides
  • the trapezoid and flips
  • the tan rhombus and turns
If not, explain how the block can be used to create a tessellation.

10 coins are worth 72¢. What could they be?

Combining Different Pattern Blocks   Creating tessellations using regular polygons

Work with a partner.

1. Tape 2 different blocks together.
   Will the new shape make a
   tiling pattern?
   Trace your pattern on paper.
   Did you use slides, flips, or turns?
   Make a different pattern
   • using the same blocks.
   • using a different pair of blocks.

2. On your paper pattern, outline the
   2 joining shapes.
   Name your new shape.
   Outline every new shape in your
   pattern. Make sure there are
   no gaps.

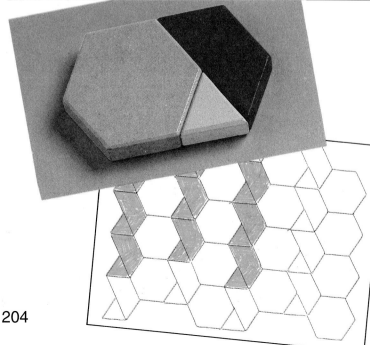

3. Tape together 3 blocks. Make a
   tiling pattern.
   Trace your pattern on paper.
   Make a different pattern
   • using the same blocks.
   • using a different combination
     of blocks

4. On your paper pattern, color any
   2 or 3 joining shapes to show a
   new, bigger shape.
   Name your new shape.
   Color the tiling pattern made
   with these shapes.

Take your pick

CHESS MOVES

A knight on a chessboard can slide in these 4 ways.

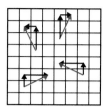

How could the knight move from A to B? A to C?

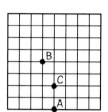

BUT HOW?

Triangle ABC was moved to the position marked as triangle DEF. Which angle corresponds to angle A? to angle B?
Which combination of slides, flips, or turns could have moved the triangle that way?

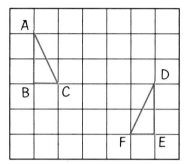

ALPHABET

Which capital letters can be turned a half turn and still look the same?
Can any be turned a quarter turn and still look the same?
What about small letters?

TESSELLATING TRIANGLE

Use a combination of regular pattern blocks to create a triangle with one line of symmetry.
Create and color a tessellation.

COUNT THE SQUARES

Where can you place a Mira to see
10 squares?   8 squares?
6 squares?   7 squares?

Make up other problems. Post them on the bulletin board for your classmates to solve.

Are there more multiples of 7 between 548 and 650 or between 748 and 850?
Tell why.

Making Traffic Signs

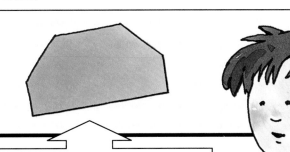

You can make a symmetric sign by folding a piece of paper and cutting out half of the shape around the fold.

What traffic sign will this look like when it is unfolded?

How can you check without making it?

Why will it be symmetric?

The fold line is called the **line of symmetry**. Why?

Use paper, scissors, and a Mira.

1. Which of these signs can be made by folding a piece of paper and cutting half the shape? Make them.

 EXIT 17   MAXIMUM 80

Which signs could have been made by folding in a different place?
How many lines of symmetry do they have?

2. Some signs can be made using a double fold.
Predict what shape these will be when they are cut out and unfolded.

Make them to test your predictions.
How many lines of symmetry do they have?

3. Which of these signs could be made using a double fold? Explain.

4. How can you use flips to determine whether a shape has line symmetry?

206

Name something that
- is true about every rhombus but not every rectangle.
- might be true about every rectangle but not every rhombus.

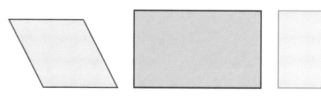

Sorting Triangular Sails

Analyzing, constructing, classifying triangles by side measures

Cut these lengths of straws:
- three 6 cm long
- three 8 cm long
- three 10 cm long

Use the straws to make these sails. Trace the triangles onto grid paper. Label the side lengths.

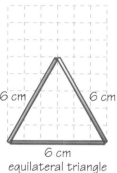

6 cm   6 cm

6 cm
equilateral triangle

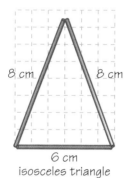

8 cm   8 cm

6 cm
isosceles triangle

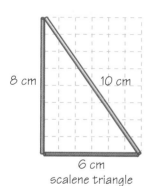

8 cm   10 cm

6 cm
scalene triangle

1. Make a different **equilateral triangle**. Trace it onto grid paper. What are its side lengths?

2. Make a different **isosceles triangle**. Trace it. What are its side lengths?

3. The **scalene triangle** could be called a **right scalene triangle**. Explain what **right scalene** means.

4. Which of the 3 types of triangles are symmetrical? Which has more than one line of symmetry?

Work in a group.

5. Use your 9 straws and grid paper. How many of each type of triangle can you make? What are the side lengths of each?
   - equilateral   • isosceles
   - scalene   • right

6. On grid paper, draw a picture to explain why a **right isosceles triangle** is impossible to make using your straws.

7. Are all equilateral and isosceles triangles symmetrical? Draw several of each and test for symmetry.

Find 8 ways to fill in the boxes so that the product has a 7 in the hundreds place.

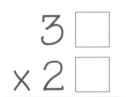

Drawing Secret Shapes

Determining minimum information to draw 2-D shapes

Janet's class is playing a guessing game. Janet drew a secret shape and then made up a list of clues. The first student in her group to guess the secret shape correctly from the clues will earn the number of points for that clue.

This is Janet's secret shape.

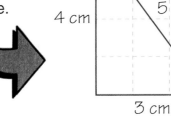

Here are Janet's clues.

1st Clue	It's a triangle.	100 points
2nd Clue	One side is 3 cm long.	90 points
3rd Clue	One side is 4 cm long.	80 points
4th Clue	One side is 5 cm long.	70 points
5th Clue	It's scalene.	60 points

1. Do you think it's possible to earn 100 points? 90 points? Explain.

2. Both Trevor and Kyle guessed after the 3rd clue. Explain why they should have waited for the 4th clue.

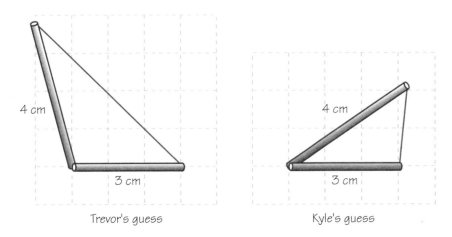

Trevor's guess   Kyle's guess

3. Why might you call the 5th clue extra?

4. Janet considered changing the 4th clue to "It has a right corner.". Explain why it would still be possible to earn 70 points.

Work with a partner.

Use straws and grid paper to help guess each shape in Problem 5-7. For each
• tell the greatest number of points you can earn.
• tell what clues are extra.

5.

1st clue	It's a triangle.	100 points
2nd clue	It's equilateral.	90 points
3rd clue	Its perimeter is 15 cm.	80 points
4th clue	One side is 5 cm long.	70 points

6.

1st clue	It's a triangle.	100 points
2nd clue	One side is 5 cm long.	90 points
3rd clue	One side is 4 cm long.	80 points
4th clue	It's isosceles.	70 points
5th clue	Its perimeter is 14 cm.	60 points
6th clue	The 3rd side is 5 cm.	50 points

7.

1st clue	It's a square.	100 points
2nd clue	One side is 5 cm long.	90 points
3rd clue	Its perimeter is 20 cm.	80 points

8. One side of a triangle is 2 cm and the other side is 3 cm. Do you have enough information to draw it? Explain.
If not, which clue below would you need to draw the triangle? Explain why and then draw the triangle.

• It has 3 sides.   • It has one right corner.   • It's scalene.

9. Explain why you could use either Clue A, Clue B, or Clue C to draw a rectangle.

Clue A   The perimeter is 16 cm and 2 sides are 5 cm each.
Clue B   The perimeter is 16 cm and 2 sides are 4 cm each.
Clue C   Two sides are 5 cm each and 2 sides are 4 cm each.

Decide if there is more than one possible shape for each set of clues in Problems 10-13. If so, make up another clue so there is only one possible shape.

10. a square with a perimeter of 36 cm

11. a rectangle (not a square) with a perimeter of 36 cm

12. an equilateral triangle with one side length 6 cm

13. an isosceles triangle with one side 5 cm and another side 8 cm

14. Draw a secret shape. Make up a list of clues and points and then give it to a classmate to solve.

There are 100 multiplication facts from 0 X 0 to 9 X 9.
What fraction of the products (0 — 81) is less than 10?
between 20 and 30?

Cutting Symmetrical Solids

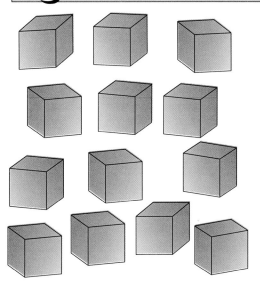

Nikki has created a **symmetrical solid** using centimetre cubes.

1. What do you think **symmetrical solid** means?

When you can draw a reflection line across a figure, you can say that figure has **line symmetry**. One half of the figure is a reflection of the other.

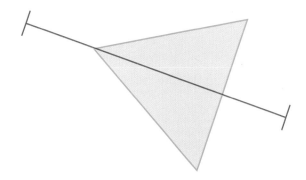

2. Draw a different symmetrical figure. Use a Mira to find the line of symmetry. Can you find more than one?

3. Use 24 centimetre cubes to create Nikki's solid.

A solid has **plane symmetry** when you can cut it into two identical halves.
One half is a reflection of the other.

4. Use a Mira to "cut" your solid into two identical halves.
   What do you see when you look through the Mira?
   Draw and describe the shape of the **plane** where the solid was "cut".
   Could you have "cut" the shape into two halves another way? Explain.

5. Make another symmetrical solid using cubes. Use a Mira to check for plane symmetry.
   Draw the shape of the plane.

6. Make a solid with cubes that has at least two planes of symmetry. Draw and describe
   each plane.

7. Use Plasticine to make a symmetrical solid.
   • Use dental floss to cut it into two identical halves.
   • Draw and describe the shape of the plane.
   Could you have cut it another way?

8. Choose three of these solids to model with Plasticine.
   • Find at least one plane of symmetry for each.
   • Have each group member try to find a different plane
     of symmetry for each.
   • Draw and describe the shape of each plane.

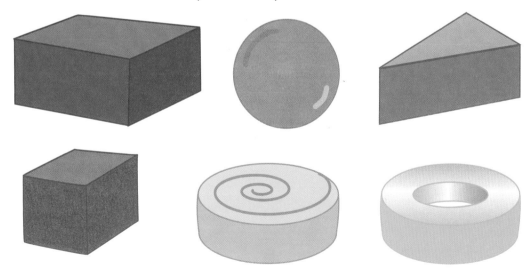

9. Where in your community do you see symmetrical solids?
   Would you say that all, most, or some human-made structures have
   plane symmetry? Explain.

$4 + 2 = 6$ and $6 \times 1 = 6$
or $6 \div 1 = 6$

Score a point.

Throw a die three times.
Use any operations with the three numbers to try to get an answer of 6.
Score a point if you get 6. The first player to get 6 points wins.

Drawing Solids

Each shape can be the front face of a prism.

Which prism would you find easiest to draw? Draw it.
Compare yours with those of others who drew the same prism.
What about the drawings make them look like prisms?

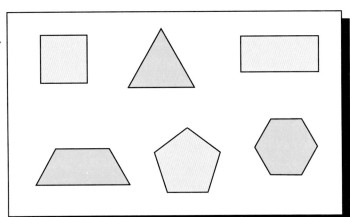

Work with a partner.

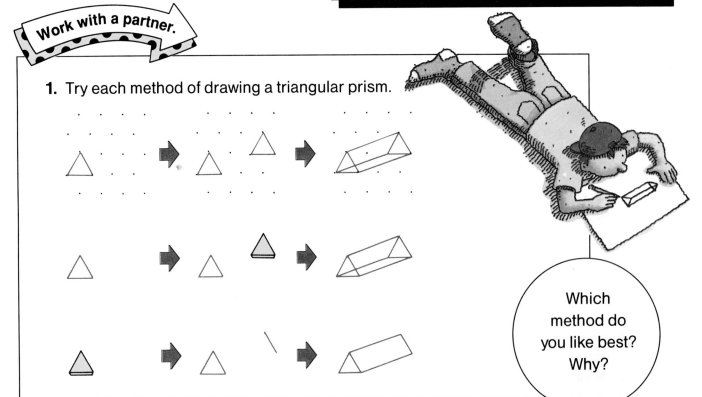

1. Try each method of drawing a triangular prism.

Which method do you like best? Why?

2. Use your favorite method to draw at least two other prisms.

3. Try drawing a cylinder, a cone, a pyramid, and a sphere.
Compare drawing each of these solids to drawing prisms.
What is the same? different?

Try this problem before going on.

MYSTERY SYMBOLS

Extend this pattern.

$$ 83 \quad \delta 6 \quad P9 \quad SM2 $$

Nathan's group solved this problem by finding a pattern.

Each symbol is symmetric.
We drew the lines of symmetry.

The parts to the right of the lines are the numbers 3, 6, 9, and 12.
These are multiples of 3.
Then we continued the pattern.

What is the twelfth symbol in this pattern?

 Work in a group.

Solve these problems by finding and extending a pattern.

HIEROGLYPHICS

Explain this pattern.
What are the next 5
designs?

EMS

Continue the pattern
with 2 more designs.
How many M's are
in the 8th design?

ANGLES

The first diagram shows angle BAD.
The second diagram shows angle BAC
and angle DAC. There are three angles
altogether.
How many angles are in the third
diagram?
Continue the pattern until you can
determine how many angles will be
in the 8th diagram.

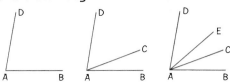

1. Which flip line goes with which flip image of the green triangle? Why?

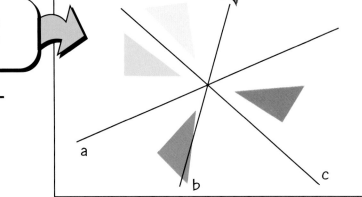

2. Suppose the letter F is turned a quarter turn clockwise about the point. Draw what it would look like.

3. Describe the red triangle in two ways. Which of these are not slide images of the red triangle? Explain.

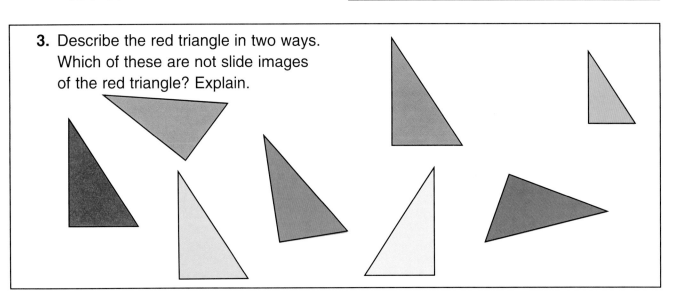

4. Use the square and trapezoid blocks to make a tiling pattern. Record your pattern.

5. Make a shape with line symmetry using
   • pattern blocks
   • a Mira
   • folding and cutting
   Do any of your shapes have more than one line of symmetry?

6. Use 16 cubes to build a symmetrical solid. Draw at least one plane of symmetry.

7. Describe the number pattern. What could the 10th number be?

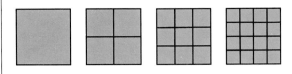

Play each game in a group of 2, 3, or 4.

Point Plot

- Each player labels a 6 by 6 coordinate grid using the colors of the dice that will be used.
- Take turns rolling the dice to get an ordered pair.
- Plot that point.
- The first player who can create a shape with symmetry by joining 3 or more plotted points wins the round.
- Play 5 rounds.

Example

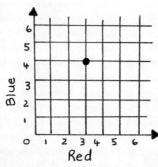

Slide, Flip, and Turn

- Each player colors half a square to form a triangle in the top left square of a 5 by 10 grid.
- Take turns spinning the spinner.
- Follow the directions to decide where to move.
- Move your triangle if possible.
- The first player to get to the bottom right square wins.

Example

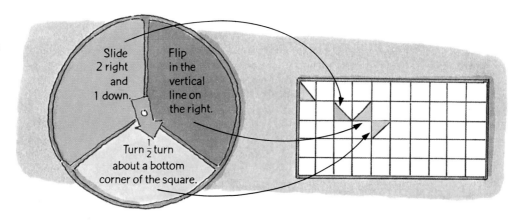

215

Take Your Pick

HOLEY MIDDLE

Make a cube with Plasticine. Make a cylindrical hole through the middle of it.

Describe or draw the shape of at least two different planes of symmetry.

TURN TO SLIDE

Think about how you might move a heavy piece of furniture by yourself.
Then show or tell how two turns could have the same result as a slide.

SQUARE PATTERNS

This series of shapes made with squares forms a number pattern if you count all the squares you can see.
Explain the number pattern.

Draw squares to show another number pattern.
Explain your pattern.

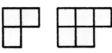 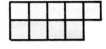

3   6   9   12

DIGITS

Examine the digits.
Describe the symmetry of each.

IS EQUILATERAL RIGHT?

Can an equilateral triangle be a right triangle? Investigate using toothpicks and grid paper. Explain your findings.

Make up other problems. Post them on the bulletin board for your classmates to solve.

1. How do you know that the blue triangle cannot be the flip image of the red one?

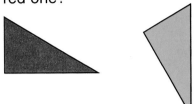

2. What motions does this strip pattern show? Create another strip pattern that shows slides and turns.

3. Why do you think tiles are not usually circles? Design a tile to use with a circle to make a tessellation. Record your pattern.

4. Trace this diagram. Then draw slide arrows to connect vertices of the yellow kite with the matching ones of the green kite.
   What do you notice about the slide arrows?
   What solid shape does your diagram look like?

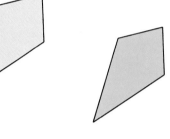

5. Describe each triangle. Describe the symmetry in each.

6. Does a trapezoid pattern block have plane symmetry? Explain.
   Draw its plane of symmetry. Is there more than one?

7. Describe how this pattern is made.
   How many sections could be in each of the next two diagrams?

8. For which shapes would you need only one measurement to draw? two different measurements? three different measurements?
   • square   • scalene triangle   • rectangle (not a square)   • equilateral triangle

217

Thinking Back

How are circles, squares, and equilateral triangles the same? different?

Can you tell whether a slide, flip, or turn has been performed when you look at the right scalene triangles? equilateral triangles? Explain.

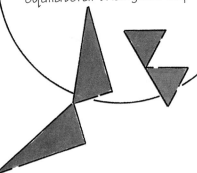

Write a paragraph describing what it would be like if you didn't have plane symmetry.

Use this picture to relate line symmetry and flips.

Why do you think most real world tiles are square?

What questions do you still have about symmetry and motion geometry?

218

Investigating Games

The Great Car Race

- Place 12 cars (counters) on the START line.
- Toss 2 dice and find the sum.
- Move the car with that number one space forward.
- Continue until one car reaches the FINISH line.

Does this seem like a fair game? Explain.

Predict which car number would win most often.

Play the game several times.

Keep a record of each winning car number.

How good was your prediction?

What games do you like to play? Which do you play the best?

What Can You Do With Tangrams?

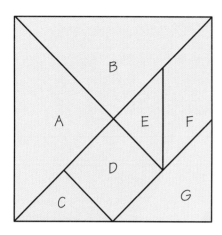

The Tangram Puzzle is an oriental matching game invented thousands of years ago by a man named Tan. The 7 Tangram pieces are shown here assembled in a square.

1. Examine the 7 pieces in the puzzle. Describe the shapes.

The pieces can be combined, without overlapping, to make other shapes. Pieces E and C can be combined to make a triangle.

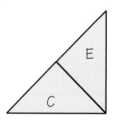

2. Combine E and C to make these shapes.
   Trace around each piece to record your puzzle.
   • a square   • a parallelogram

Trace around each piece to record your solution to each puzzle.

3. Make a triangle using each of these numbers of Tangram pieces.
   • 3 pieces   • 4 pieces   • 5 pieces

4. Make a square using each of these numbers of pieces.
   • 3 pieces   • 4 pieces   • 5 pieces

5. Make these shapes using 3 pieces.
   • parallelgram   • rectangle (not a square)

6. Use all 7 Tangram pieces to create this design.

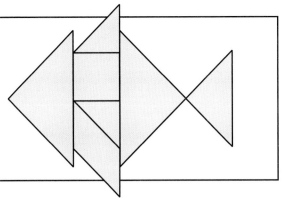

7. Create your own design using all 7 pieces. Trace around each piece to create a puzzle. Give the puzzle to a classmate to solve.

You can make the puzzle difficult by only tracing the outline.

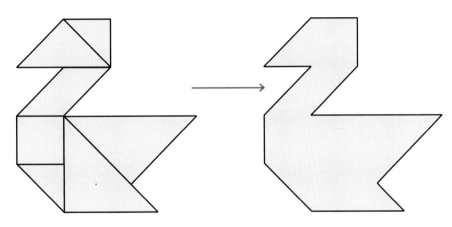

8. Create a puzzle using all 7 pieces. Keep a record of the solution by tracing around each piece.
Give only the puzzle outline to a classmate to solve.
You might give clues by showing where one or more of the pieces go.

Did you know...?

The world's largest jigsaw puzzle covered about 4800 m² and had 43 924 pieces. It was assembled on July 8, 1992 in Marseille, France.
▶ How does the puzzle's area compare to the area of your classroom?
The average size of each piece was about 0.1 m² or 1000 cm².
▶ Find several objects in your classroom which have about the same area.

221

HOW Can Shapes Be Arranged on a Gameboard?

The Last Triomino

- Take turns coloring a triomino on a 5 × 5 gameboard.
- No triominoes can overlap.
- Continue until no more triominoes can be colored.
- The winner is the player who colors the last triomino.

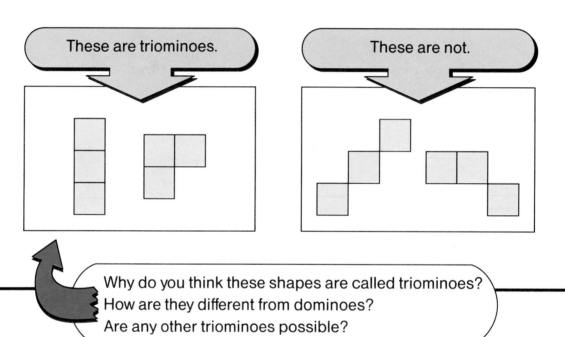

These are triominoes.

These are not.

Why do you think these shapes are called triominoes?
How are they different from dominoes?
Are any other triominoes possible?

1. You are blue and it's your turn. Describe where to color a triomino to ensure that you will win.

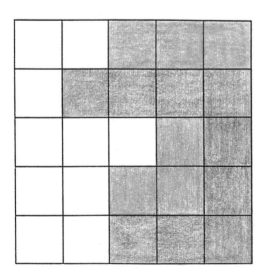

2. Use the motions slide, flip, and turn to describe pairs of triominoes.

If you flip the yellow triomino, you get the purple one.

3. Play The Last Triomino several times before answering the rest of the questions.
Keep track of who goes first and who wins.

4. Is it possible to fill all squares on the gameboard? Explain.

5. What sizes of square gameboards could be completely filled if only one shape of triomino was used in a game?

6. Use each motion once to describe a different pair of triominoes in one of your games.

7. What fraction of the games did the player who went first win? second? Do you think it's better to go first or second in this game?

8. Play this variation of The Last Triomino several times using each shape.

Variation: Each triomino colored must be a slide image of the previous one. Keep track of who goes first and who wins.

9. Is it better to go first or second when playing the variation?

10. These are tetrominoes. There are three others. What are they?

Make up and play a game using tetrominoes. What size of gameboard did you use?

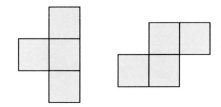

Did you Know...?

The slowest game of competitive chess ended in a tie and took 15 h to play 56 moves.

▶ About how long did each move take?

HOW Much Money Will Be Won?

Money Path– A Game of Chance

- Place a penny on START.
- Toss another penny twice.
- Each time it lands heads, move the marker penny 1 space to the right.
- Each time it lands tails, move the marker penny 1 space up.

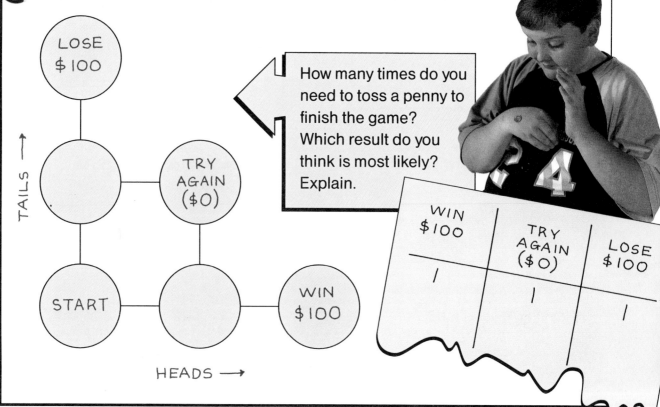

How many times do you need to toss a penny to finish the game? Which result do you think is most likely? Explain.

WIN $100	TRY AGAIN ($0)	LOSE $100
1	1	1

Work in a group.

Compare your results with other groups.

1. Play Money Path 8 times as a group, taking turns tossing and moving the pennies. Tally the results. How good was your prediction?

2. After what combinations of tosses did you land on TRY AGAIN? WIN $100?

3. Make a bar graph to show the number of times each result happened.

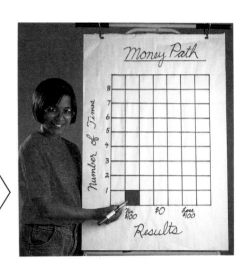

4. Find the average amount of money won or lost.

5. For this gameboard, how many times do you need to toss a penny to finish the game?
How would you complete this gameboard so that you are most likely to break even?

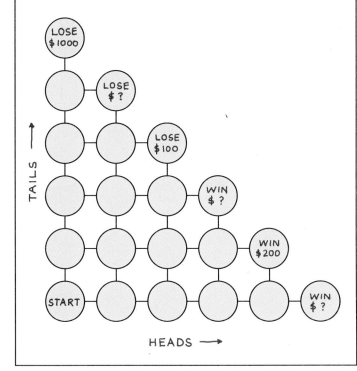

TAILS →

LOSE $1000

LOSE $?

LOSE $100

WIN $?

WIN $200

START

WIN $?

HEADS →

6. After what combinations of tosses would you land on LOSE $1000? LOSE $100?   WIN $200?

7. Play this variation of Money Path 32 times. Tally and then graph the results.
Compare the shape of this graph to the shape of your first graph.
Find the average amount of money won or lost.

8. How would you rearrange the results on the gameboard so that you are more likely to win money than lose it?
Play your variation of Money Path and check.

9. Design a similar game using a different number of spaces and different results.
Tell whether you are more likely to win or lose money.
Play your game and check.

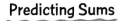

Predicting Sums

Shuffle nine cards. Then place them face down in a row in front of a group of 3 or 4. Before a pair of cards is turned face up, ask each student to predict whether the sum of the two numbers will be
- 7 or less
- 8 to 12
- 13 or greater

Repeat the entire process several times and keep a tally of the sums that occur. Which sums occur most frequently? Tell how you could make this into a game.

Paper, Rock, and Scissors

Flash one of these hand signs at the same time as a friend.

paper   rock   scissors

Keep a tally of wins, losses, and ties using this scoring system.

Paper covers rock.   Rock dulls scissors.   Scissors cut paper.

Play the game 20 times. What is the probability that you will both show the same hand sign so that no one wins a game?

Tic-Tac-Toe

How many different ways are there to win at Tic-Tac-Toe?
Play several games. Do players win more often when they start first? when they place their mark in the centre?

Trying Tangrams

Use all 7 Tangram pieces to create a shape with the
- least perimeter possible
- greatest perimeter possible

Make up your OWN investigation. Then post it on the bulletin board for others to try.

Thinking Back

The wheel is spun twice to get two numbers.
If the difference between the numbers is less than 8, I win.
If not, you win.

Explain why you wouldn't play this game.

Examine the 7 Tangram pieces. Describe how the 7 pieces compare in area. Explain what you did to compare areas.

Some magazines use numbers from 0 to 10 to rate video games where 0 means poor and 10 means excellent.
One game scored Graphics: 9
Sound: 10
Challenge: 10
Ask several students to rate different video games. Then tell how to rank these games.

Find a game that uses math. Show a group of students how to play it.

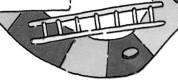

What else would you like to know about games?
Tell what you would do to find out.

227

Index

Credits

Acknowledgements

Acknowledgement is hereby made for kind permission to reprint the following material:

Excerpt from THE DARK by Robert Munsch. Text copyright © 1979 by Robert Munsch. Illustrations copyright © 1979 by Sami Suomalainen. Reprinted by permission of Annick press. Printed in 1979, revised in 1984. "Overdues" text and art by Shel Silvertein from A LIGHT IN THE ATTIC by Shel Silverstein. Copyright © 1981 by Evil Eye Music, Inc. Reprinted by permission of Harper Collins Publishers. Excerpt from THE HALF-BIRTHDAY PARTY by Charlotte Pomerantz. Text copyright © 1984 by Charlotte Pomerantz. Illustrations copyright © 1984 by DyAnne DiSalvo-Ryan. Reprinted by permission of Clarion Books/Houghton Mifflin Co. All rights reserved. Excerpt from CLOUDY WITH A CHANCE OF MEATBALLS by Judi Barrett and Ron Barrett. Text copyright © 1978 by Judi Barrett. Drawing copyright © 1978 Ron Barrett. Reprinted with permission of Atheneum Publishers, an imprint of Macmillan Publishing Company. Illustration from THE TURN ABOUT, LOOK ABOUT, THINK ABOUT BOOK by Beau Gardner. Copyright © 1980 by Beau Gardner. Reprinted by permission of Lothrop, Lee & Shepard Books, a division of William Morrow & Company, Inc.

Every reasonable precaution has been taken to trace the owners of copyright material and to make due acknowledgement. Any omission will be gladly rectified in future editions.

Photographs

page 154, Comstock/M. Stuckey; page 159, left, Comstock/Eric Hayes; page 159 right, Comstock/H. Armstrong Roberts/M. Koene; page 166, Comstock/William Marin Jr.
p. 201 top, Comstock/Pierre St. Jacques; p. 201 bottom, Comstock/ E. Otto; p. 200 Unilock Ltd.;
Product photos pages 44-225 by Tom McCrae
All other photos by Ray Boudreau

ST. PETER SCHOOL
720 - 56th STREET S.E.
CALGARY, ALBERTA